SECRETS
FROM THE
INNOVATION ROOM

SECRETS FROM THE INNOVATION ROOM

How to Create High-Voltage Ideas That Make Money, Win Business, and Outwit the Competition

KAY ALLISON

Art by David Buscher

McGraw-Hill

New York   Chicago   San Francisco   Lisbon   London
Madrid   Mexico City   Milan   New Delhi   San Juan
Seoul   Singapore   Sydney   Toronto

The McGraw·Hill Companies

2 3 4 5 6 7 8 9 0   DOC/DOC   0 9 8 7 6 5 4

ISBN 0-07-144375-4

McGraw-Hill books are available at special quantity discounts to use as premiums and sales promotions, or for use in corporate training programs. For more information, please write to the Director of Special Sales, Professional Publishing, McGraw-Hill, Two Penn Plaza, New York, NY 10121-2298. Or contact your local bookstore.

 This book is printed on recycled, acid-free paper containing a minimum of 50% recycled, de-inked fiber.

Library of Congress Cataloging-in-Publication Data

Allison, Kay.
    Secrets from the innovation room : how to create high-voltage ideas
that make money, win business, and outwit the competition / by Kay Allison.
        p. cm.
    ISBN 0-07-144375-4 (pbk. : alk. paper)
    1. Creative ability in business. 2. Organizational effectiveness.
        3. Success in business. I. Title.
HD53.A423 2004
658.4'063—dc22

                                                        2004012342

CONTENTS

ACKNOWLEDGMENTS

I would like to acknowledge and thank the following people who have inspired, encouraged, and supported me in creating this book:

- John Donicht, my husband and business partner, for his unflagging encouragement, love, and consistency. You make my dreams and ideas become reality. This book is proof.
- Claire, Christian, and Anya, my darling, beautiful, playful children whom I adore.
- To my clients, who encourage me and expect me to experiment and grow.
- Dan Sullivan, my business coach, who gave me the tools to package my intellectual capital and the community that made sure it happened.
- My Coach2 buddies, who keep me on track and challenge me to keep up.
- Robert Stuberg, Rob Hart, and David Buscher, who are packagers extraordinaire.
- My students at Northwestern University, who were an engaging and challenging audience as I developed this material.
- Sensei Jeff Kohn, who challenged me to break my first board at my black belt test and who has challenged and coached hundreds of my clients and students to do the same since.
- To my creative inspirations: Natalie Goldberg, Laurie Beth Johns, Jean Houston, SARK, Julio Ollala, and John Kao.
- My sisters, Jan and Sue, and my mom and dad, Bev and Clare, for setting me up to be highly ambitious.
- To my vigilant and encouraging editors: Kelli Christiansen and Janice Race. Thanks for guiding this newbie through the process.

INTRODUCTION

My name is Kay Allison, and I make my living by helping people have ideas.

Many people I've worked with consider themselves to be intelligent, well educated, and open to new ways of working, yet when they are faced with the prospect of having to generate new ideas, they say with resignation, "Oh, I'm not creative." Creative people have new ideas all the time, right? New concepts spring fully formed from their heads with ease. "I can't do that!" people insist.

Why is the creative process such a mystery? Why are we so quick to believe that creativity is magical, a talent that very few are given? It's easier to stand back, to let other people—the ones who are creative—have the ideas.

One of the first things I tell my clients is that I didn't start out as a creative person. I didn't believe I was creative at all.

My older sister, Jan, was an artist. I was not. She had the idea of creating artwork on the cement walls of the basement of our house in a suburb outside of Chicago. On one side of the basement, she painted a series of panels; each had a piece of poetry surrounded by beautiful images, each in a distinctly different style from the others.

After I saw what Jan had done, I couldn't wait to try it myself. I badgered my parents into giving me a part of the basement to paint. My side of the basement had a single wall . . . and I couldn't come up with a single idea.

I kept looking at Jan's work and wondering what I should do. Other thoughts kept creeping in: Was I good enough to do this? Would my wall be as good at hers? Where should I start? How could I make my wall as cool as hers but different enough to reflect my own personality?

Without a plan in mind, I began painting. I painted "Kay's Place" at the top of the wall, and under the title I painted my garden. It came out as a wall of dorky-looking flowers. They were boxy and amateurish, with thick stems and no perspective. I looked at my painting and thought, "I'm a failure. I can't do this. I never should have tried. I'll never be as creative as Jan."

I tried many things (singing, acting, playing the cello), diving into each with a great deal of enthusiasm and a modicum of talent.

However, despite my energetic attempts, nothing I tried led to success. I had to be realistic and realize that I wasn't going to earn my living as a singer, an actor, or a cellist. So, I went into advertising. In advertising agencies, there is a department of people who are called "creatives." I was not in it.

Clearly, I wasn't creative; I didn't have the title.

And yet I kept being asked to have ideas, and to have them fast.

"YOU'RE LOOKING IN THE WRONG PLACES"

When I had been working at a big ad agency for a year, an executive at an international Fortune 500 company asked me to write a presentation on how to market "mature" brands. This guy worked in the floor wax category. With more women working and the rise of no-wax flooring, this guy's business was tanking fast. Here I was, labeled "uncreative," but expected to produce ideas that had enough power to stanch the losses this guy was facing. There was a lot on the line here. This client's career would be affected. His company's profits and stock price would be affected. My agency's relationship with this client would be affected. And, not least, my career would be affected.

I asked my bosses, "What do I do? Where do I start?" They directed me to look at examples in other packaged goods categories and to learn lessons from other people's experiences. I remember gathering all kinds of information—case histories, consumer surveys, videotapes of other people's advertising. I worked lots of hours. Then I went back and showed my bosses what I was doing.

"You're looking in the wrong places," one of them told me.

"Well, where should I look?" I asked.

"Just keep working. Ask the Information Center for more articles."

I raised my eyebrows, asked for more articles, stayed late. I wrote some kind of presentation that showed what companies in similar positions had done. Then I drove to another state to make my presentation to my client. I explained what had worked for lots of other companies, but the client kept asking me, "So what does this mean for me?" and "Now what should we do?" He was interested in something more revolutionary than what I'd given him. He wasn't interested in the lessons of the past; he wanted to know how to get to the next revolution.

What I remember most about the presentation was not being able to help my client create the kind of ideas that would drive sales, revolutionize his category, and connect with consumers in a new and powerful way. Copying other people was not going to enable me to answer my client's questions.

I survived that presentation, but it left me with some burning, basic questions: What makes an idea a good idea? How do you consistently generate good ideas? How do you find that magic "x factor" that makes an idea stand out?

My entire career, from director of new business development to innovation consultant, has been focused on the answers to those questions. I have been on a quest for ideas, a search for the source of creativity. Not in some abstract, vague sense; I knew there had to be a way of thinking that led to good, new, fresh, practical ideas. And I was on a quest to find out what it was.

SO WHY THIS BOOK?

As you hold this book in your hands, you can tell that it looks different and feels different from most of the other books you've probably run across on this subject.

This is a book about thinking in new ways, but it's also a book about action. I'm going to ask you to do things: Carry the book around with you; draw on the pages (I've left room for sketches and notes and bursts of inspiration); rip the pages out. There's no magic list of answers that you can find by flipping to the back of the book. I can suggest the steps for you to take. You have to commit to actually taking them.

You see, I've learned that just thinking about a problem may not be enough to develop a creative solution. Throughout this book, I've created experiences that, if you participate in them, are opportunities for you to have powerful, high-voltage ideas that will have the power to rock your world.

Most people don't think they can have ideas that will change things. I know I sure didn't think of myself as creative. The fact that, after my initial failures at being creative, I've found a way to produce high-voltage ideas on a consistent basis tells you that there is hope.

One of the things that has most inspired my search for creative solutions is an idea I got from one of my most influential teachers, Dan Sullivan of The Strategic Coach. Dan says that we have a fundamental choice in every situation: We can create, or we can complain. Think about that for a moment, and then make a choice about how you'll approach each challenging situation in the future.

Creativity is applicable in more than just the business world. This book will show you—if you make the choice to create rather than to complain—how to generate ideas that can and will change things for the better.

Let's get started.

EXERCISE

DESCRIBING CREATIVITY

What do you think of creativity? Right now, before you begin a book dedicated to the topic, it's time to get to the heart of your current beliefs. Consider it a gauge that pinpoints the starting point of your journey.

On the back of the page, write or draw everything you really believe about creative people. Do you think they're geniuses? Airy-fairy? Impractical? Inspirational? Weird? Powerful? Wear too much black? Be as detailed as you possibly can, and get it all out!

When you've written everything you can, examine the list carefully. Where did those ideas come from? Are they grounded in your experience? Something you saw on television? How attached are you to these beliefs?

What's Going On Here ¿

A person's attitude toward creativity is one of the chief factors that determine whether he or she is able to tap into it. How many of the beliefs you listed may actually keep you from accessing your own creativity, either because they don't seem worthwhile, or because they seem like something beyond what ordinary you can aspire to?

Consider your descriptions again. Would they match Thomas Edison? Benjamin Franklin? Ghandi? Steve Jobs? Queen Elizabeth the First? These are all deeply creative people who used those abilities to change the world.

EXERCISE

DESCRIBING CREATIVITY
(Continued)

STOP! <u>DON'T</u> TURN THE PAGE YET!

You just finished the first of many experimental exercises you'll find in this book. Please complete each one as you come to it, and don't read any further until you've done so. Each exercise is carefully designed to help you understand new ideas instinctively and emotionally, not just intellectually.

SECRETS FROM THE INNOVATION ROOM

1 DEFINING THE UNDEFINABLE

Let's analyze creativity.

That's a joke, right? People talk a lot about "creativity," but what exactly does that mean? The dictionary gives a straightforward definition: the ability to be original, to imagine new things and new ideas.

Businesses thirst for new ideas and always claim to be on the look-out for creative solutions to problems—you don't see anyone using the tagline "We Do Things the Old, Boring Way." Creativity in today's business world means coming up with ideas that make money, win business, and make the competition shake in its boots—ideas that have equal measures of uniqueness and relevance. The problem is that most good businesspeople are trained to be analysts: Analyze the consumer demographics, analyze your sales data, analyze the performance of your competitors. Obviously, there is great value in being smart about your business—in knowing to whom you're selling and how much they're buying.

However, analysis can only set the stage for innovation. A creative solution can't be analyzed into existence. Brilliant ideas seem obvious only after the fact—once someone has a great idea, then all the analysts can tell you exactly why it's a great idea. But the process doesn't work backwards; all the data in the world can't spontaneously produce a new idea.

To be creative is to reach out into the unknown, to imagine something that doesn't currently exist. That implies risk, and if you're a good businessperson, you're rightly suspicious of risk. Organizations thrive on numbers, on proof, on hard facts. New ideas are simultaneously desired and feared. We all want them—but where are they? How do we uncover them? Why do some businesses seem to be innovation machines? It's easy to see a good idea once it already exists, and it's easier in hindsight to see an opportunity once it's already been exploited. What's hard is developing a process that identifies opportunities and generates ideas on a consistent basis. That's what this book is dedicated to providing for you.

You could define insanity as "doing the same thing over and over and expecting a different result." Everywhere I looked, I saw companies doing just that: trying something that was successful in the past and expecting to get something new out of the process.

ARE YOU INS- ANE ??? ???

(look on the next page to find out)

EXERCISE

WHERE DO YOU GET YOUR IDEAS?

Despite the provocative question on the previous page, this exercise is not really going to tell you if you're insane. (The most I can help you there is to repeat what a friend once told me: "If you think you are, you probably aren't." Or was that the other way around!) But this *will* help illustrate your style of approaching new problems.

Imagine you've been hired to create a new brand of tennis shoe and given absolute freedom to do anything you want. Right now, before you read any further, use the space on this page to roughly sketch its appearance and list its features.

What's Going On Here ¿

What was the first thing you did when faced with this problem? Did you think about the sneakers you already own? List categories of shoes and work within those? Picture existing brands and duplicate their styles and innovations?

Or did you try to look at the sneaker in a new way? Imagine a new demographic, or try to figure out what an existing demographic wants and isn't getting? Devise features no sneaker has had before?

When you look to the past for the solutions to problems like this, or if your starting point is to accept the parameters of what's already been done to solve them, you limit your potential for innovation.

LEFT BRAIN, RIGHT BRAIN

If you're interested in creativity, then you've probably been exposed to the concept of "left-brain" and "right-brain" thinking.

The theory grew out of the work of Nobel Prize–winning psychobiologist Roger Sperry, whose study of epileptic patients showed that each hemisphere of the brain processed different types of information. Broadly put, the left brain is the objective, analytical, logical half of the brain, looking at information sequentially and focusing on individual parts rather than on the whole (remember left = logical). The right brain, on the other hand, is the subjective, intuitive, playful part of the brain; it looks at information in a more random fashion, seeing the whole rather than the parts.

The "voilà!" moments of innovation come from the right brain: You suddenly see how unrelated things connect; you see a new solution to a problem; you are struck by a new idea from out of nowhere. Monumental discoveries from penicillin to nylon to X rays were all made by accident—through the serendipitous flashes of insight that come from the right hemisphere.

But once you have that insight, what do you do with it? Here's where the left brain comes into play, giving concrete form and shape to the right-brain-inspired concepts.

If you're reading this book, it's a good bet that you are more comfortable operating in your left brain than in your right brain. The exercises throughout the book are designed to get your right brain activated: Rather than sit and wait for "inspiration" to strike, you can prime the pump and get the ideas flowing. Once you have the raw material (concepts and ideas), you can let the left brain do its thing and start editing and planning.

It's important for you to remember that you can't simultaneously be in "idea-generation mode" and in "editing/analyzing mode." One has to follow the other.

What this means is that when you're doing the various exercises in this book, you will be sorely tempted to analyze the experience as you are going through it. "Am I doing it right? Is this what's supposed to be happening? How do I know if it's working?"

In order to access your right brain with any success, you have to do your utmost to keep your analytical brain from kicking in until after you're done with the exercise.

There are explanations of why and how the exercises function and the kinds of results they can have (to satisfy the logical cravings of the left brain). But in the end, they are all trying to accomplish the same thing: to stimulate the right brain, the source of inspiration.

EXERCISE

A MENTAL PICTURE OF YOUR BRAIN

Close your eyes and summon up a visual image of the right side of your brain.

Then do the same for the left side.

Quickly sketch the image that you see. Go with the first thing that comes to mind. Don't overthink.

When I first did this exercise, I saw my right brain as a mountainside meadow filled with wildflowers and people dancing and singing.

I saw my left brain as walls lined with steel shelves. There was a steel trap on one of them, but it was covered with dust.

Nowadays, my left brain is neater and cleaner . . . but the first image is telling, isn't it?

EXERCISE

SOLILOQUY

A soliloquy is a monologue in which someone gives voice to his or her deep feelings. Shakespeare used this device a lot in his plays: one of the most famous begins, "To be or not to be. . . ." In this exercise, continuing the process of getting in touch with your existing beliefs about creativity, you're going to give voice to the right side of your brain, the part associated with creativity and intuition.

Fill in the following blanks as you believe your right brain would. Have fun, lighten up, and write down whatever comes to you. Don't censor yourself.

I am the spirit of _____

I have traveled _____

I have met _____

I have conquered _____

I have learned _____

I have tried and failed _____

I am stuck on _____

I yearn for _____

What's Going On Here ¿

What is your creativity trying to tell you? Is it anxious to be accessed and harnessed as a helpful force in your career and in your life? Is it afraid of you? Has it atrophied from neglect? Does it have a secret you don't know about? People are often surprised by what their right brain is trying to tell them— and listening is a great way to begin this journey.

LOGIC VERSUS ENERGY

We all know a good idea when we see it. A good idea grips you. There's an immediate gut reaction, a zing that makes you feel inside like, "Yes, of course! That's right. That's cool. I want that."

A zingy idea gets your attention. Ideas like that have voltage, energy, life. They have the energy to make you different. They have the power to change your mind, your imagination, even your actions. They have the oomph to change your company or your industry.

A good idea is relevant to your life. It resonates with you . . . and yet it's different enough that it didn't occur to you before. No matter what the idea or innovation, if it's great enough to change you, it has that magic combination of relevance and difference.

I've sat through too many meetings where the people in charge approved the idea that made sense rather than the idea that got a reaction from the room. In meeting rooms all over America right now, managers are arguing for the "make sense" ideas rather than the ideas with a spark of energy. In fact, the truth is that the worst idea is the one that makes sense. If you're not excited and energized by your idea, what consumer is going to be?

This is another instance of the left brain (logic) triumphing over the right brain (intuition). The majority of us live in our left brain. We've been trained to be logical people. Obviously, there's value in logic—at the right time. When it comes to innovation, the role of logic is to sort and strategize rather than to generate. Ideas that don't elicit a reaction in a meeting room are unlikely to generate a reaction in the marketplace.

Reason has a role in the innovation process; it's just not operative at the beginning. John Kao and Dorothy Leonard at Harvard Business School teach that the process of innovation can be thought of as a diamond shape: It has a divergent and a convergent side.

The divergent top of the process is driven by emotion and energy (right-brain qualities); the convergent part of the process is driven more by logic, as the left brain comes back into play. Many of my clients are much more comfortable in the convergent part of the process than in the divergent part. The

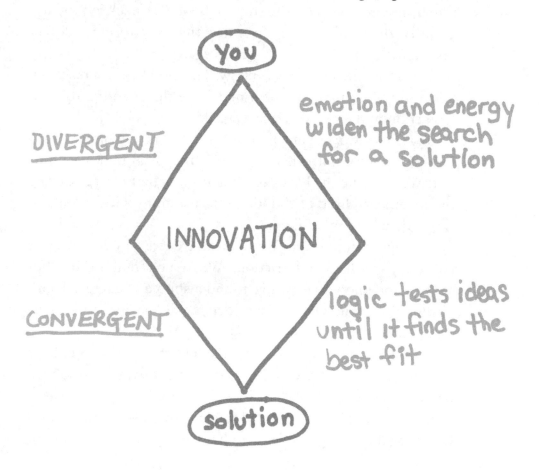

divergent part can feel uncomfortable, and that's OK. Just stay there for an hour or a day longer than you're used to, and you may be amazed at what creative genius steps forward. We need to let our logical minds take a rest on the hammock for a little while we're working early on (just as I've asked you to do with the exercises in this book).

When we let go of logic for a moment, we can be open to ideas that might not "make sense," but that get a reaction. We've all been in meetings where people react strongly to something—perhaps with a laugh, an inadvertent "mmm . . . ," scorn, anger, the hair on the back of the neck going up. Usually those ideas are the ones that get discarded and discounted.

Those are the ideas with energy. They've elicited a reaction. Some nugget in that comment may have the potential to elicit a reaction in the marketplace as well.

Do you always want to run with the raw "mmm . . . " idea? Of course not. This is where our logical minds help us out. We can take the basic, unfiltered ideas that emerge during the divergent phase of thinking and use our logical minds to shape them and mold them.

Energy is important. You can find energy by looking for paradox, conflict, and friction. When you find those "hot spots," you know that you've found a source of energy. That's fertile territory in which to start drilling, exploring, and generating ideas.

All of the innovations that have had the power to change my life have in some way given me a fresh way to resolve a paradox I'd been living with. For example, when I was a single, working mom, I wanted to hire other people to do stuff for me as much as possible (who has the time or the energy for an expedition to the grocery store every week?), and yet my kids are picky, and I'm fussy. I want it done my way.

Then Peapod introduced an online grocery shopping and delivery service that was personalized to my needs. I could order all my groceries—and specify that I wanted bananas that were really ripe—and the next day they were delivered to my third-floor walk-up condo. Everything was just the way I wanted it, yet I didn't have to do it myself. Peapod is a great resolution of conflicting desires.

I'll use various examples throughout this book, but I don't necessarily believe in studying case histories in minute detail. That path leads to my fledgling "this is the way everyone else has done it" floor wax presentation. Everywhere in our culture—in the marketplace, on television, in the movies—you can see examples of imitation substituting for innovation. Carefully putting your feet into someone else's footsteps is not the same as learning how to walk.

Instead, we're going to look beneath the surface, at the process of thinking creatively—and at the ways in which we often stop ourselves from thinking this way.

This book will help you have ideas that work because they grip people. The opportunities for having ideas that work are all around us every day. They come out of the stuff of life; they don't come from mad scientists with test tubes shut up in labs all day long. We all have situations that we accept with a shrug and a feeling that "that's just the way life is." These are the situations in which we can choose to complain or to create. They are fertile territory for powerful ideas.

2 ENEMIES OF IDEAS AND INNOVATION

If we were all fully capable of inventing novel solutions to every challenge we faced, all of our problems would be solved quickly. What I've found is that we're all held back to some degree by enemies of ideas. In this chapter, we will explore some simple ways to stop these enemies in their tracks before they shut us down completely.

"Of course," you say to yourself, "I have good ideas. I'm a creative problem solver. I'm open-minded. I'm not like those cartoon middle managers who hide in cubicles and squash any new ideas that cross their desks. No, I want to break boundaries, push the envelope.

"But—

Any of this sound familiar ???...

- Jerry the new VP isn't going to go for this one; I already know that . . .
- This doesn't sound like it fits with our company's personality . . .
- That just doesn't make sense . . .
- We should develop this one the way we did the last one. That worked . . .

Any of this sound familiar ???...

- We can't do that. This is serious business here . . .
- I know what I'm talking about; I've done this a million times . . .
- That part of it is not my job, anyway. Everybody here knows that . . .
- I just want a calm meeting here. Don't start with the stupid ideas . . .
- There isn't any time to get this done, anyway."

Everybody wants to be innovative. Nobody wants to be known as the guy who said that the lightbulb was a bad idea that would never work. The tricky thing about the enemies of ideas, though, is that you can't always recognize them.

It's ironic that many patterns of behavior and modes of thinking that work well in performing certain structured activities (test taking, for example) only get in the way when we try to use them to come up with new ideas. We're taught from an early age to know the right answer, to be polite, to be sensible, to stick with the tried and true, to try harder. It's not so easy to abandon the behaviors that we know to be "right."

The tools and techniques that many companies employ provide an exquisitely sophisticated snapshot of what *is*; however, those same tools and techniques simply don't work to show what *could be*. Many companies rely on expensive and exquisitely detailed reports that show every nuance of brand sales, product usage, brand-switching behavior, cost sensitivity, and so on. What these reports don't show is how the power of an idea could change things.

In my work, I've encountered the same enemies of ideas over and over. Some of them turn up everywhere, while others seem more specific to particular organizations. In the pages that follow, we'll look at the ten most prevalent enemies of ideas that I've experienced.

The first step to eliminating these barriers is to recognize them. Which ones are most present in your work? In your life?

ENEMY ONE

I'm AFRAID of how I'll look to someone else.

This is a big one, but it's a hard one to admit to. No one is willing to own up to being afraid. Cautious, prudent, perhaps even conservative, but not afraid. In the corporate world, admitting fear is tantamount to admitting failure. It's just not done.

But the fear is there, even if it's well disguised.

We all remember only too well the feeling of being in front of the class and making some kind of mistake. Your face reddens; your adrenaline starts pumping; you feel sweat trickling down the back of your neck. It's not an experience that anyone wants to repeat.

We go through elementary school, high school, college, graduate school, and up through the ranks of companies, always with an authority figure that we have to please. Even CEOs have to answer to Wall Street. And underneath our well-coordinated businesswear, somewhere there's a fourth grader who has resolved never to look stupid in class again.

Maybe you don't call it fear; how about anxiety? Apprehension? Stress? Worry? When you don't feel secure in a situation, you won't allow yourself to risk. You can imagine pitching a new idea to your colleagues, clients, or supervisors and getting the eye roll, the puzzled look, the dismissive comment ("interesting, but not what we're going for here").

Fear is paralyzing. The fear of being judged, of looking stupid, of being wrong, of failing, of taking the blame—it's lurking just beneath the surface, in the clever disguise of caution. When you can't put the full force of your enthusiasm and passion behind a new idea, that idea will be dead on arrival.

One thing I've learned is that whatever I focus on grows. So if I focus on the anxiety that gnaws in my belly, it gets so big that it's paralyzing. On the other hand, if I focus on what my next appropriate action should be, it gets me into motion.

EXERCISE

WHAT ARE YOU AFRAID OF?

This is a very important exercise. Cover this page with a list of what you're afraid of. Rational, irrational, it doesn't matter. This is the place to let your fears loose. Get them all out. Use the back of the page. Study each one carefully, because it may lead you to others.

EXERCISE

WHAT ARE YOU AFRAID OF?
(Continued)

EXERCISE

WHAT WOULD YOU DO?

On this page, make a list of all the actions you would take if you didn't have the fears you just listed. What would you do if you could set aside those fears for a moment? If I told you to borrow my faith that it will all work out, what action could you take today?

What's Going On Here ¿

You'll find that most of these enemies of ideas and innovation, no matter what they're called, are about fear—fear of how you'll look to others, fear of embracing the unknown, fear of looking at the world through unfamiliar eyes. Fear is insidious and will always seek to hold you back. Your personal fears are nurtured by your unwillingness to face them or even to name them. This exercise can be the first step in examining your fears and their inevitable consequences, and the first step to overcoming them.

TURN BACK TO YOUR
LIST OF FEARS...

RIP IT OUT OF THE BOOK!!!

DO IT!!! I'M NOT KIDDING!!!

* Now make a schedule of accomplishing the actions you just listed.

Don't focus on fear. Focus on action!!!

ENEMY TWO

Having a "fixed" vs. a "fluid" point of view.

All of us, especially those of us who are ambitious and driven, are used to advancing our own point of view. We have a particular way of seeing things, and the more focused and specific that vision is, the more successful we are.

This kind of mindset can work brilliantly in a debate, but it doesn't serve you as well when you're trying to see fresh solutions to issues or opportunities. From any one perspective, you can see only 180 degrees of the world. What you need is to see the full 360.

It's easy to forget that there are many people involved in any business transaction, all of whom have different needs and opinions. If you can shift your point of view and get inside the skin of someone else—your consumer, your supplier, the guy from R&D—you'll be able to dramatically expand the number of possibilities that you can see.

There is the hidden fallacy that if you can somehow push your own particular point of view, amplify it, and make it loud enough, everyone will fall into line. If you consider any monopoly (The Ford Motor Company back in the day of the Model T, for instance), you'll find this mode of thinking: You can have a car in any color, as long as it's black. A one-size-fits-all approach dismisses the validity of any alternative opinions.

This may seem obvious when you think about extremes (for example, a dictatorship versus an open society), but it can be hard to spot in yourself. When you're thinking about a particular problem, really peel away the assumptions you're making. "We don't need to make cars in different colors. Nobody cares what the car looks like—it's a utilitarian appliance. All people want is to get from one place to the other."

Closely related to this way of thinking is, "We've always done it this way" (see Enemy Seven). Sometimes you need to ask yourself, "If I were going into business to compete with my own company, where would I start? Whose needs are we not serving? Why do people prefer this feature in my category? Why is that important to them? How does it fit into the rest of their lives?"

The Wright brothers, inventors of the first successful heavier-than-air craft, took nothing at face value. Every inventor who was working on building an airplane at that time was relying on the same tables of aeronautical data that had been compiled by an earlier pioneer in the field. The Wrights challenged conventional thinking and began from scratch, questioning every assumption that their predecessors had made.

When they were trying to solve a problem, the brothers would each take one side and fiercely debate the issue, then they would change sides and argue the opposite viewpoint just as vigorously. They tested every theory this way, ensuring that they saw every issue from every angle.

To a conventional thinker, it may seem that conceding the existence of opposing views will weaken your own convictions. Paradoxically, the ability to see many sides of a situation allows you to come up with the most viable solutions. Adopt a diplomat's mindset: What is the person on the opposite side of the table thinking? What can you learn from that person?

EXERCISE

GET TO KNOW SOMEONE

My friend Teresa Easler asks her clients to write a list of everything they know about the person they're communicating with, including a list of the things that they can appreciate about that person. After all, the person is someone's child, brother, friend. Think about someone in your company, about your competition, about your customers.

What's their background? What's their history?

What's important to them? Why are they at this meeting?

What motivates them?

What's missing for them?

What are their hopes and fears?

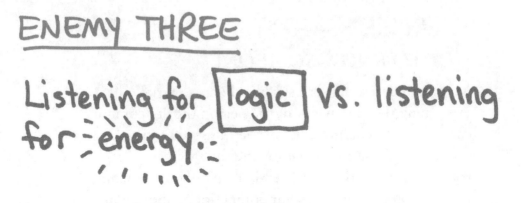

Most of us write down the logical things that are said in meetings: "That seems like the sensible course of action." There are always ideas that seem perfectly rational, seem to solve the problem at hand, and yet have no "spark" in them. They are the equivalent of middle-of-the-road political candidates: They satisfy all the basic requirements, but they won't get anyone up out of their chair to go to the polls.

How many times have you seen a movie (or even a "coming attractions" trailer for a movie) and realized that you know exactly how everything will turn out? A leads to B leads to C . . . all the necessary plot points are covered (car chase! love scene! heart-tugging ending!), and the movie unspools in a completely predictable fashion. Everything makes sense, but nothing is exciting. The best moments come when something unexpected enters the story—not something completely random, but a twist, a jolt that pushes the action out of the predictable.

In a meeting, the "logical" idea is often one that can be completely understood immediately. You know how everything will turn out. There are no surprises. The idea with energy behind it is often a surprise—and it gets a reaction.

You can see how listening for logic easily goes hand-in-hand with the first enemy of innovation, giving in to fear. If you're looking for no risk, then every idea should be rational, by-the-numbers, and completely unsurprising. If you're only listening for logic, then any idea that's new can immediately be picked apart and found to be unworkable (many times, we'll do this in our heads before a new idea has a chance to make it out into the room).

When you're listening for energy, write down the thing that makes the room react. What makes people laugh? Groan? Get angry?

Write down all the ideas with colored pencils, markers, or crayons. Tepid ideas get tepid colors; energetic ideas get written down in big, bold letters. Draw circles around them; decorate them with stars; follow them with exclamation points! The ideas that make a stir in the meeting room have a nugget of energy that will get a reaction from your customers as well.

The secret of listening for energy is having the patience to figure out how to make the energetic ideas doable. It requires being able to engage in "what-ifs" without dismissing anything as impossible.

Hold on to those ideas that spark a reaction, even if it's not immediately clear how they can be put into practice. How can we expect to get a reaction from the marketplace when we can't get a reaction from our team?

This brings us back to the idea of left-brain–right-brain cooperation. Use the right brain to make the "leaps of logic" that generate ideas, and use the left brain to find a way to make those ideas work. One side supplies the raw material; the other side edits, shapes, and polishes. Just don't try to make the left brain do the right brain's work. Let energy come first, then use logic.

EXERCISE
KEEPING TRACK OF THE ENERGY

When you go to your next meeting, bring a box of colored pencils. Every time somebody says something that gets a reaction in the room, write it down in color.

At the end of the meeting, go back and see how you can work with those ideas to make them doable.

ENEMY FOUR

The belief that doing the <u>same</u> action, only **HARDER**, will get a different result.

This may be true when you're working with a hammer and nails, but it isn't true in meetings. The moments when people make breakthroughs—when the right idea just pops into someone's mind—often come when they're relaxing after a period of intense concentration.

If you ask most people when breakthrough ideas have come to them, you'll find that they've been driving, or in the shower, or walking—performing a simple task that keeps part of their brain occupied but frees the "back part" of their brain to rummage around and dig up new ideas.

So, don't fall into the trap of hammering away at a problem for too long. Make it a regular practice to schedule in 15-minute breaks after you've been working for, say, two or three hours. Outlaw any business talk during the break. Step outside for a breath of fresh air or a walk around the block.

Bring in a yoga instructor who can show you a few asanas that you can do easily in your work clothes.

Sometimes you need to change the texture of your normal work session to get new and better results. Try changing the players involved—besides the usual team members, invite an unusual expert to participate (for instance, an author, a student, or an authority with a differing point of view). The group dynamic will always shift when there is a new presence in the room. Break from whatever your usual meeting procedure is—disrupt the usual patterns. Play word association games; solve puzzles together; put Legos on the table.

Really look at your work environment—chances are it's a completely left-brain-focused space. Conference rooms with straight lines, inconspicuous overhead lighting, colors that don't assert themselves—these are all fine for logical, straight-ahead thinking, but not so conducive to thinking in new ways.

Break away from the usual. Hold your meeting in a different physical environment—a theater stage, a funky loft, or a rec center.

This enemy also shows up as "the same information, only louder, will get different results." Ad agencies make this argument to their clients all the time: "The campaign would work if you put more money behind it." And sometimes that's true. Other times you've got to change what you're saying, how you're saying it, or where you're saying it in order to get through to someone in a new way. I've also had bosses who seemed to believe that the louder they said the same thing, the better the results they'd get. Not true.

Again, remember that the definition of insanity is doing the same thing over and over and expecting different results.

EXERCISE

TAKE A BREAK!

Set the book down. Your crucial assignment is to . . .

Draw a picture.
Go for a walk for 15 minutes.
Do some stretches.
Listen to some music you enjoy.

See what new ideas pop into your consciousness while you're gone. Write them down and share them with your team.

ENEMY FIVE

Addiction to answers.

When my older daughter, Claire, was born, I distinctly remember thinking, while I was lying there holding her for the first time, that finally I'd know all the answers, just like my mom did. Imagine my surprise and dismay when I realized that that degree of certainty did not come along with the baby!

Most businesspeople know lots of answers. We all got good scores on our SATs. We knew the answer to "where do you want to be in five years?" when we were interviewing for jobs. We know the latest P&L projections. The problem is that needing to always know the answers doesn't allow us to wonder about the questions.

Think about the standard interview questions for a moment. Chances are you've been on one or both sides of this interaction. Have you ever wondered, why are *these* the questions? Has anyone ever given a fresh, inspired, unrehearsed answer to the question, "Where do you want to be in five years?"

This addiction to answers is a natural response to the way we're taught. You come into a situation (a classroom) in which the same process happens day in and day out: You are presented with a question, and you are expected to produce the answer, an answer that someone else already knows (in fact, chances are it's an answer that everyone else in the class also knows). The answer is on the teacher's copy of the test or hiding in the back of the book. Your entire scholastic career is built up of numbers—percentages that reflect how many questions you answered correctly.

Linear thinking and problem solving are good skills to have, but they sometimes act as blinders. We obediently search for answers to the questions, but it doesn't occur to us to wonder about the larger picture. When you're asked in second grade about how many apples Johnny has if he starts with five and gives two away, all you are expected to say is, "Three." You aren't asked to think about who Johnny is, why he has so many apples, whom he's giving them to, or why this simple math question is framed as a story about an imaginary kid with pretend apples.

You can see a pattern developing with all the enemies of innovation: relying on unthreatening logic, accepting boundaries without question, not wanting to risk challenging the status quo. Everything leads to the celebration of the obvious and the dull.

We have to shake ourselves loose from the deep inner conviction that, somewhere, there is a Big Book of Answers that holds the solution to every problem. If this book were a book of answers, there would simply be a list of case studies with their corresponding solutions—but all that does is deliver the end result without examining the process that brought the result about. There is no flipping to the back of the book here to find the answers. Instead, there is a continuing process of reconditioning yourself to think about situations in a new and broader way.

I asked one of my clients to create a board game that represented and operated by the rules that governed the way the business currently worked. Then we went in and methodically helped the client create a whole new go-to-market strategy for a new brand. In my own business, I've done the same thing. The "rule" of the focus-group facility business is that you interview consumers in sterile environments, so that you do not influence them in any way. What I found was that sterile environments yielded sterile responses. So in my facility, the Energy Annex, we created Natural Habitat interview rooms, designed to make the people we interview feel relaxed, comfortable, welcomed, and at home. Not surprisingly, they are more forthcoming when that's the way they feel.

Chasing the answer doesn't allow us to pretend or imagine or to be in awe. Think about the situation at hand in broader terms than "problem/solution." Before you hunt answers, look for all the questions.

EXERCISE

MAKE THE RULES/BREAK THE RULES

Imagine that the situation that you're looking for a creative solution for is a game with a set of rules. Write out the set of rules.

> Who are the players (as defined in the rules)?
> What is the balance of power? Who has the information, and when do they have it?
> Who gets involved in the process? At what point?
> How does each player behave in a given circumstance?

EXERCISE

MAKE THE RULES/BREAK THE RULES
(Continued)

Now question the rules. How could you shift them? What actions would you have to take to shift the balance of power? What would happen if you changed who the players were or when people got involved?

What's Going On Here ¿

Rules are very comforting, but they don't encourage inquiry. They are logical, not energetic. They are convergent, not divergent. They are answers without questions.

Every game—that is to say, every situation in life—has rules. The logical part of our mind wishes to impose them and respect them and follow them, without ever understanding them or questioning them.

When it's your turn to make the rules, what limitations do you impose? It's our own built-in rules, beliefs, and expectations that limit what's possible. As Nelson Mandela said, "Who are we not to be great?"

ENEMY SIX

The belief that if the subject is IMPORTANT, we need to be SERIOUS.

I tell my clients, "What we're working on here is critical . . . it will affect the company's stock price, people's careers, the division's P&L. And if we're serious, we're screwed." This always gets a laugh.

Sometimes a certain amount of pressure can be invigorating, but can you honestly say you've ever had a good idea when you were trapped at your desk, sweating bullets, and thinking about the incredibly high stakes involved in your project?

It's a different, more subtle form of fear, but it's still paralyzing. Think about a more extreme case: Imagine the plight of someone who is trapped in a panic-inducing situation. From the comfort of distance, we can wonder, "Well, why did he run *toward* the fire/deadly cobras/radioactive zombies? I certainly wouldn't do *that*." Scale down the panic to the stress-suffused atmosphere in your office, and you can see that under the crushing weight of seriousness, the best decisions aren't being made. When your tunnel vision is setting in, you can't evaluate or even recognize a good idea.

When the stakes are high and you desperately need a powerful idea, that's the best time to try something light and playful. Even the most senior executives seem relieved when they can lighten up—if only for 30 minutes.

Creativity and imagination require that we play, that we be relaxed and free. Being overly serious can stifle even the most creative spirit, intimidating it into never speaking out.

EXERCISE

BE FANCIFUL

Fill in the blanks. Seriously.

"What if . . . "
"I wonder . . . "
"Why don't we . . . "
"If only . . . "
"I wish . . . "
"If I had a magic wand, I'd . . . "
"In a perfect world . . . "
"Wouldn't it be great if . . . "
"How could . . . "
"It might be that . . . "

ENEMY SEVEN

Relying on your previous experience to create something <u>new</u>.

Most businesses look to their competitors for benchmarking or case studies. But too often, it's easy to succumb to insular thinking: "I've been in the widget business for 10 years; I know the widget market like nobody else. I've studied how Acme Widgets and Universal Widgets run their shops. I understand what the widget consumer needs."

That may be laughable, but insert your top product in place of "widgets," and it starts to have a familiar ring.

There's a short distance between using your experience and judgment as a guide and simply trying to repeat your past successes with no new element. That's safe evolutionary thinking instead of *revolutionary* thinking.

To use a movie analogy, movie sequels strain to duplicate the success of the original blockbuster. They have the same stars, the same stories, the same special effects. But here's the rub: What was "Ooooh! Ahhh!" the first time around is "Ho hum" the second, third, fourth, and fifth times.

Revisit Enemy Two, having a fixed rather than a fluid point of view. Are you trapped in thinking like an industry giant rather than a hungry start-up? Are you creating movie sequels to products rather than thinking up new genres? You can see how this enemy of innovation fits into the pattern of all the others: no-risk logical thinking.

I encourage my clients to look beyond rather than within their own industry. Direct your focus outside the world of widgets, and think about what feedback you might get from people who are far removed from your particular field.

EXERCISE

GET ADVICE FROM THE OUTSIDE

Imagine that you're talking to Gandhi. What would his advice be?

How about Eminem?
What about Hillary Clinton?
General Patton?
The guy who used to be your best customer?
The woman you wish were your most loyal client?

List three more people of your choice from different walks of life. What advice do they have for you?

ENEMY EIGHT

"It's NOT MY JOB!"

It's everybody's job to be creative and to participate in life. Refusing to take part in the creative process immediately closes a mental door and becomes a self-fulfilling prophecy: "I never have any ideas."

This is yet another enemy of innovation that is rooted in fear. After we've avoided risk for long enough, we become apathetic. The creative muscles atrophy from disuse, and we forget that we ever had them. We label ourselves as "not creative," and then our creativity dies.

We all have a mental composite of ourselves constructed of labels, some of them positive and some negative. Once we have decided that a label fits, we limit our behavior to conform to it. We live those labels as if they were facts (scientifically provable), rather than judgments that we might be able to shift.

So, it's not your job? Make it your job. Take the risk. Take responsibility for your own creative development. Take ownership of the creative things you've done in the past. Seize opportunities to flex your creative muscles in the future.

What it all boils down to is that you need to rip off that "not an idea person" label. The only thing that makes that label true is your own belief in it.

EXERCISE

OWN YOUR CREATIVITY

It's list-making time!

The lists don't have to be orderly and neat. Jot down anything you can think of under the following headings. What are . . .

- All the great ideas I've ever had in my life:
  (Think about decisions like whom to marry, where to live, a great outfit you put together, the lighting fixtures you chose for your kitchen, your idea for a great vacation or outing, your way of distracting a crabby toddler.)

- What I've created in my life:
  (Meals, great family dynamics, enough financial well-being to support yourself/others, a successful team at work.)

EXERCISE

OWN YOUR CREATIVITY (Continued)

- What I've designed:
  (This could be a new report at work, a new way of making kids' school lunches, a process to disengage from work at the end of the day, a Christmas letter . . . anything.)

Look at those lists. Does your tally match your assessment that you're not creative?

What's Going On Here ?

Reminding yourself of how you've been creative in the past will open the doors wider to future creativity. Remember, the point of this book is that creativity doesn't have to be some abstract pie-in-the-sky artistic endeavor. It really has some very practical results—results that you can generate if you take it on as part of your job.

ENEMY NINE

Avoiding FRICTION.

I'm an idea person. Given any situation, I have hundreds of ideas about how to make it better, more fun, more effective, more innovative. Nothing stops me cold like someone who shuts down my idea fountain.

"No, that's a bad idea."

"That'll never work because . . . "

"We did that before, and it failed."

It makes me absolutely crazy.

At the same time, I'm not a detail person or a process person. So while I might have a vision of what the end looks like, I'm pretty clueless about how to actually get there. I love, love, love people who'll say to me, "Yes, cool idea. Help me brainstorm some ideas about how to solve this potential obstacle."

When it's framed that way, I'll have some more ideas about how to overcome that barrier. The point is to use the energy derived from friction to propel a process forward, rather than having it shut somebody down completely.

If you ever study improvisational comedy, you'll find that one of the basic rules is, "Never say no." A comic scene needs to have conflict, but if one of the participants blocks the way, the scene is doomed. For instance, a basic comedy setup might be a person with 12 items going head-to-head with an express-lane cashier. If the shopper says, "Fine, I'll go somewhere else," and leaves the store, then obviously the scene is over. If either participant refuses to engage in the developing idea, then there's no point in continuing.

On the other hand, nobody wants to watch a scene in which two people agree about everything. Conflict provides interest; the key is that the conflict mustn't shut the process down.

You can see shades of all the other enemies of innovation here: fear of failure; listening for logic instead of listening for energy; "that's the way we've always done it"; "it's not my job." It's a pervasive way of thinking that is difficult to break out of until you recognize it in its many forms.

In idea-generating meetings, it's important for the most senior person in the room to sincerely ask the participants for their help in creating new solutions to the given business problem or opportunity and to empower them to question the rules (even if she's the one who made them up). If this doesn't happen, the session can turn into nothing more than everyone toadying up to the senior person to see who can score the most points. When it does happen, it keeps the door open, allows friction, and creates the kind of energy that can propel a project forward. Remember, friction is good. Conflict is good. It makes things interesting.

And it provides the energetic fuel to power up new ideas.

EXERCISE

KEEP THE DOOR OPEN

When you're voicing an objection to someone else's ideas (or your own), try saying, "Yes, I hear you. *AND* let's brainstorm some new solutions for a potential hurdle I'm anticipating." Or, "The things I like about that idea are . . . Now let's build something around those qualities."

Think about an idea (whether yours or someone else's) that was recently rejected out of hand. Write down things that could have been said to consider the possibilities behind the idea.

ENEMY TEN

No Time!!!!

We have deadlines to meet, kids to pick up, email messages to return, voicemails building up . . . let's hurry this up! Gotta go, gotta run, see you later.

It seems inefficient to take 15 minutes at the beginning of a meeting to get people emotionally engaged, to set the context appropriately, to set the right mood, to discuss how we're going to interact. And yet, if you take that 15 minutes, the meeting will have a life of its own.

Also, you have to protect against interruption. The creative process builds momentum and picks up steam. Ideas start flying, and breakthroughs happen. This buildup of energy can't take place if cell phones are ringing, people are ducking out, or supervisors are poking their heads in "just to see how the meeting's going."

The creative process needs to be approached in the same way you approach physical exercise. You don't run into the gym in your business suit and hop right on the Stairmaster. (Well, perhaps you do, but . . .) There's a series of steps to the ritual: You enter the gym, you proceed to the locker room, you change your clothes, you stretch, you begin to exercise. Your mental focus changes. The preparation gives you time to turn your attention and energy to the task at hand. Once you begin your workout, you don't undercut it with interruptions every other minute. If you don't build momentum, no benefits are gained.

The process of opening yourself up to new ideas is no different—there is stretching involved. Just as in working out, warming up and allowing yourself sufficient time to focus and prepare is crucial. Begin each project by deciding how long you'll spend on the divergent part of the diamond, then how much time you'll allot for the convergent side. Have team members discuss what it would take for the project to exceed their expectations and what the obstacles or dangers facing the project are. Appoint a team member to be the voice of the client or customer throughout.

You'll have better ideas, the work will get done faster, and people will be happier and more engaged. It works like magic.

EXERCISE

MAKE TIME FOR CREATIVITY

Schedule a few hours to work on a project away from the office.

Shut off the phones; don't answer email; turn off your pager.

Tell your administrative assistant, your staff, and your colleagues that you have an important meeting outside the office, and you'll be back in three hours.

Take your laptop or your notebook or your sketch-book, sit in a place where you feel comfortable, and write your presentation, design your brochure, write out your process plan—whatever your big project is that needs attention.

EXERCISE

Let's take another quick look at the enemies of innovation.
They're listed on the back of this page.

Mark the two enemies that your current work environment
is most guilty of. More often than not, they aren't obvious . . .
they creep silently into the corporate culture like carbon
monoxide: invisible, but deadly.

Now for the harder exercise: Mark the two that you,
yourself, are most guilty of.

Now flip to the back of the book to find the correct answers.
(How many of you fell for that, even for a brief second?)

The next step is to share this exercise with a colleague,
ideally one whom you don't know very well. (Why someone
you don't know very well? To help you combat Enemy Two,
the fixed rather than fluid point of view, and putting yourself in
someone else's mindset.)

After you're both finished, share your responses. Talk about
what the experience was like for you, not about what your
answers were. (We're taking a stab at the addiction to answers
here. It's important to be conscious of the process at this point,
not the product.)

You'll often find that you have more in common than you
might suspect.

Start a meeting with this exercise. Ask each person to circle
which enemy she's most guilty of and then share that with
someone she doesn't know well. You'll be amazed at how the
barriers melt away. (It's like throwing water on the Wicked
Witch of the West.)

EXERCISE
(Continued)

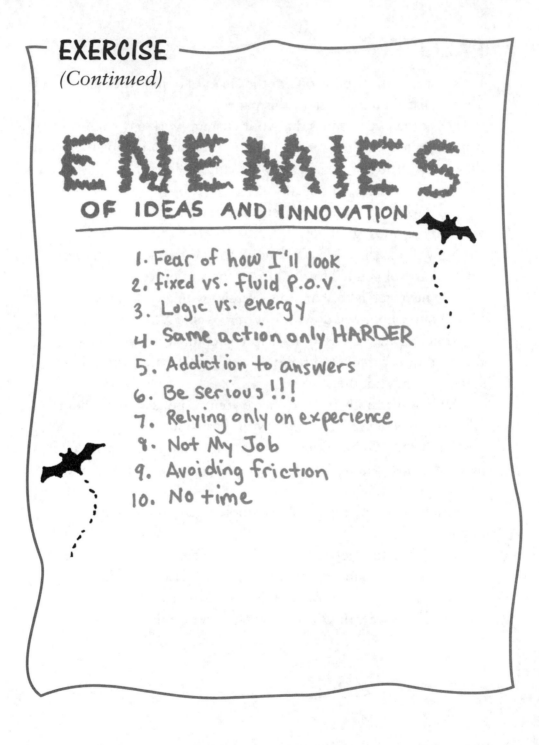

ENEMIES
OF IDEAS AND INNOVATION

1. Fear of how I'll look
2. fixed vs. fluid P.O.V.
3. Logic vs. energy
4. Same action only HARDER
5. Addiction to answers
6. Be serious !!!
7. Relying only on experience
8. Not My Job
9. Avoiding friction
10. No time

Keep this "10 worst enemies" list where you can see it, both when you're working alone and when you're in meetings. The first step in combating these pitfalls is to recognize them when they appear. Acknowledge that being "sensible, cautious, and responsible" has helped you before, but you don't need it now.

It all comes back to fear. You're at the chalkboard. You have the chalk in your hand. It's your turn to answer.

Take the first action and start to move.

3 ASKING QUESTIONS

So, we've looked at what creativity is and what the major obstacles to creativity are. The next step, you might think, would be to jump in and start dreaming up solutions to whatever problem you might be facing.

Ah, but not yet.

If you're trying to generate new ideas in business—new advertising concepts, new product development, brand revitalization—you're dealing with very specific kinds of problems. You're not in exactly the same situation I found myself in when I was trying to concoct the world's most brilliant basement mural to outshine my sister. There are other people involved—clients and consumers—and finding a new idea is going to depend on how well you know these people. All energized ideas come from providing a fresh solution to a common, pressing problem. So the first step is to ensure that you know how your client/customer/prospect/consumer really experiences that problem and what it means to her or him. We need to experience the problem fully from these people's points of view, not from our own. That's where to start.

And before we go looking for answers, we left-brainers should be really sure that we've defined the questions correctly. Your consumers aren't thrilled with your new lemon-scented widget? Maybe you think you know why. Your market research seems to tell you why. But don't be too sure just yet.

Most market research is excellent at telling you what is (or what was yesterday) and how that compares to how things were earlier. This leaves it up to you to figure out what could be, what possibilities exist. Creativity is as much about framing the questions as it is about generating solutions (we're not going to say "answers" because we're not addicted to finding answers—right?).

If you talk to the people you're selling to in a different, more generative way, you'll get relevant, energetic information that will be much more illuminating than the results of dry market research. Talking to people in this way is much easier (frankly) than sitting at your desk trying to think up something revolutionary by yourself, and it can lead to much more exciting results.

Everyone else's problems are your opportunities. Really.

Repeat after me: Everyone else's problems are your opportunities to create innovative solutions.

Your ideas have to connect with the people you serve in powerful new ways if those ideas are to be successful. So do *not* start with the proverbial blank sheet of paper. There's nothing more intimidating and nothing more uninspiring. First, figure out whom you serve (or want to serve).

By the way, Bob Dylan was right. We all serve somebody. Whose issues do you care the most about? That's whom you should serve. So, once you've figured that out, I'll show you how to listen to those people in a creative way that will help you generate winning ideas. Get out and talk to people! That's where to start.

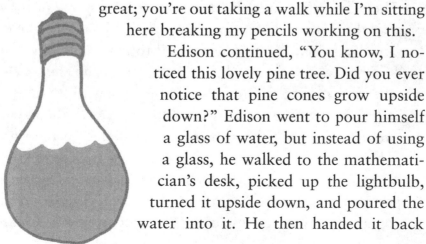

A STORY BREAK

There's a story about Thomas Edison that has made quite an impression on me.

There was a mathematician who had the job of figuring out the volume of the lightbulb. Since it was an unusual shape, neither a sphere nor a cylinder, this wasn't an easy proposition. This man was very intelligent and well-educated, and he went about his task very conscientiously. According to the story, he consulted all his textbooks, he tried different formulas, he consulted all of his professors, and he consulted his professors' professors.

The mathematician was hard at work when Thomas Edison came in from a walk and said, "You know, it's beautiful out there." And the mathematician was thinking, Well, great; you're out taking a walk while I'm sitting here breaking my pencils working on this.

Edison continued, "You know, I noticed this lovely pine tree. Did you ever notice that pine cones grow upside down?" Edison went to pour himself a glass of water, but instead of using a glass, he walked to the mathematician's desk, picked up the lightbulb, turned it upside down, and poured the water into it. He then handed it back to the mathematician and said, "Here, measure the volume of the water."

With any problem, I always advise people to turn it upside down. Look around you; get inspiration from nature; go for a walk; go outside. Don't just look at the task at hand.

BEING AND DOING

This chapter is all about asking questions in a way that will help you identify the fertile soil for innovation. There are two important components to this: the *doing* part and the *being* part. Many people will tell you the sorts of things you can do (tips, tricks, or techniques), but they don't pay much attention to how you can be—that is, what is the way of being that you should adopt in order to allow yourself to really be present in a room with someone and experience what it's like to be inside that person's skin.

How should you be in order to ask questions and really hear and comprehend the answers that you get?

The way we'll frame the discussion of questions in these pages is through the unique focus groups that I have developed for my clients, but don't limit yourself to that context as you explore the issue for yourself. I use these ideas all the time— whether I'm talking to my husband or talking to my clients or interviewing consumers. As someone once said, the key to all progress is asking the right question (doing) in the right way (being).

Most of the time, we think of action as straightforward. A man walks across the room and picks up a glass of water. A woman speaks to her employee. But actions themselves are usually the tip of the iceberg. Since most communication occurs nonverbally, actions can be multilayered and carry great weight.

In the film *All About Eve*, there is a scene in which Bette Davis's character argues with her boyfriend. Again, one would think that performing this scene would be straightforward: In an argument, one is angry. But strangely, for take after take, the actress couldn't convey the right emotion. She could "do" the argument, but she had trouble with the "being." Finally, the director told her to seem during the argument as if she were dying to eat a piece of candy from a nearby bowl. The resulting scene sizzles with tension.

EXERCISE

SEPARATING BEING FROM DOING

Watch a video of your favorite movie and take notes. What are the actors doing, and how do they provide texture to the scenes by being? How would the scenes change if the actors took the same actions but were directed to be another way?

Really watch other people in meetings. Is there coherence between what they're saying and how they're being? What if they shifted their way of being? Would it change the meaning of what they're saying?

LOOK AROUND AND LISTEN

Many people believe that the secret of getting great ideas is listening to that mysterious inner voice, that guiding intuition that offers brilliant mental suggestions to all those who know how to listen to it.

Well, yes and no.

That is the voice of your creativity, and it should always be honored, but uninformed creativity can often send you down the wrong path . . . the path of irrelevance. So when you're looking for that as-yet-undiscovered idea that will make you (or your client) rich and happy, don't start by looking inside yourself. Look around at the outside world first. Delve into other people's lives and psyches.

I love Frederick Buechner's definition of vocation; it's a true gauge of a great idea, as well. He said that your vocation is when "your deep gladness and the world's deep hunger meet." Likewise, a great idea happens when what you have (tangible and intangible) meets the world's deepest hunger.

So where do you begin if you want to have a great idea? Stop counting the ceiling tiles, examining your navel, or staring at that blank sheet of white paper. Get out and talk to the people you're trying to reach! You can pick up so much in a face-to-face conversation with a consumer or a client, either one-on-one or in a well-crafted focus group, if you know how to listen to what that person is saying and process that information accordingly. The rest of this chapter is devoted to helping you develop proactive listening, the kind of rich, active listening that will create the fertile soil for great ideas.

SPRINGBOARD MENTALITY

Of course, it's easy to think, "I have an open mind. I'm ready to listen." Unfortunately, we all have a bit of built-in arrogance. We've made it this far in life by trusting our instincts and imposing our own particular set of perceptions on the world around us. It's hard to let go of this.

Each time I conduct an interview, I try not to walk in with predetermined answers. I've always got some hypotheses that I'm curious about, but I never walk in with a particular result that I've already decided upon: "The answer is Y" or "These people are Z." I go in with a springboard mentality: "You show me what's cool here and where the energy is." And when I do pinpoint the energy, that mindset allows me to turn on a dime and pursue it, often springing off in directions that I could never have predicted or imagined.

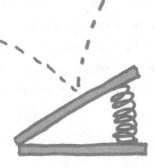

THE ENERGY YOU BRING

Before I ask questions of a consumer or a client, I ask questions of myself first. Who do I want to be? What parts of my personality do I want to bring to this situation? In my case, I always want to be warm, friendly, funny, inviting, encouraging, and empathetic.

Every dialogue has two sides. Every interview is a transaction, an exchange. What will my half of the transaction be? What am I bringing to the table? What is the energy that I will evoke? Because energy transforms you—you aren't just acting, you're being.

So that's the first element of asking questions: Pay attention to how you are, what your presence is, what your energy is like. Think about how you are being in addition to thinking about what you're doing.

EXERCISE

ENERGY DOESN'T LIE

Someone once told me that people can see through words, but that energy doesn't lie. Try these three experiments on energy and a springboard mentality and see if you can discover the truth in that statement:

First, try saying hello to the same person in three different ways (at three different times). Say it angrily, suggestively, in a friendly manner . . . how does the person react to each greeting?

Next, take this one step further. Begin conversations with three different strangers. These can be cashiers, neighbors you've never spoken to, or just people on the street. You can talk about anything you want to—talk about the weather or a sports team, or ask for directions—but the catch is, all the conversations have to be about the same topic, and you must start each one with the same opening line. The only difference is that you'll approach each person with different energy. You can be gruff, enthusiastic, timid, overbearing, or anything else you can think of. Notice how the other person reacts to you in each case—the differences that each kind of energy brings.

Finally, find three other strangers or people that you don't know well. Start conversations on different topics, and this time, approach these people with an encouraging and empathetic attitude that gets them talking. The trick

EXERCISE

ENERGY DOESN'T LIE (Continued)

here is to listen for the energy. They'll doubtless show some sort of spark when the conversation swings around to an area they're passionate about. Pick up on that spark and fan it into a flame. Follow the energy and see where it leads. Afterward, plot a trajectory for each conversation, pinpointing where it started and the direction it sprang off in once you teased out that spark.

HOLD THE SPACE

When I'm asking questions, I try to be conscious of all aspects of the experience, not just the information I'm trying to get at. There's a human aspect to the process of interviewing, a way of making people comfortable so that they will open up and feel free to talk. The phrase I use is "holding the space." When I "hold the space" for these people, I'm present with them; I'm focused and interested and attentive.

I hardly ever take notes when I'm interviewing. I can't really be present if I'm scribbling notes. I make tapes, which are transcribed later. I nod, I supply all the appropriate body language, and, most importantly, I allow silence. I give people the room they need if they are to consider. I hold the space.

I also try to have the experience create value for the focus-group participants. Sure, they make 50 or 100 bucks for their time, but I want them to walk out of the focus group with a sense of clarity that they didn't have before. I want them to have the feeling that somebody has actually valued what they had to say. When people feel valued, they open up more. They're more enthusiastic. They're more ready to give thought to what you're saying. It's a two-way street: When people feel valued, they provide value back to you.

THE BIG "SO WHAT?"

So what are we listening for? While we'll get into this more in the next chapter, here are a few hints up front.

1. *Pay attention to anything that the person you're interviewing has chosen to complain about.* Remember the comment in the introduction about how, in any situation, you have to choose whether you're going to complain or create. If someone's chosen to complain about something, it could be because that person feels powerless to create a better solution or situation. What could you create that would take away the complaint?

2. *Look for ideas that are antithetical to each other.* For instance, someone might tell you in one breath, "I want to be healthier," and in the next, "I don't want to change any of my habits." The friction between those two ideas held by the same person is the potential energy for innovation.

3. *Notice dis-coherencies, that is, things that are not coherent with each other.* For instance, get really interested when someone is a very controlled person in almost every detail of his life but is wild in one particular area. Ask lots of questions about what's going on there. I've gone shopping with moms who are putting Pop-Tarts into the cart, while at the same time telling me that they're concerned about the amount of sugar their kids consume. It's fascinating to hear them talk about that incongruity. For many, their real concern is getting their kid to eat something (*anything*) before the child leaves for school. It's the lesser-of-two-evils choice. Aaaahhhhh, could there be an opportunity to create a breakfast product that kids will actually eat that gives them some protein so that they can concentrate longer at school?

EXPLORING THE CONTEXT

Besides being present and alert, I always want to have the attitude of being open and curious—keeping a fluid point of view, in defiance of Enemy of Innovation Two.

One of the goals of this kind of consumer exploration is to explore the context of the answers. You may think you know why people are saying what they're saying, but as soon as you start to explore beyond the obvious, you discover the underlying connections, the way people put things together for themselves.

When I interview someone, I make sure that each response leads to another question:

> Why is that important to you?
> Where are you coming from with that?
> That's really interesting. Explain to me what you mean
> by that.
> How does that fit into your life?
> Have you encountered that before? How have you
> solved that in the past?

With each subsequent answer, you learn more and more about the layers of context in the particular situation. People are motivated by contextual things, by the push and pull of their immediate environment. Most interviewers don't pay attention to context; they just pay attention to, "How do you spread your cream cheese on your bagel?" They never think about the woman they are interviewing beyond her cream cheese preferences. They don't progress to wondering, where is this woman coming from? Does anybody do anything nice for her in her life? Does she get even two minutes a day to do anything for herself? What secret luxuries does she allow herself?

When you fully understand the context, you'll think about cream cheese differently. You can shake yourself free of your preconceptions about your product and the people who are using it, and begin to open your mind to new ideas.

We'll talk in Chapter 5 about how effective marketing shifts the emphasis away from the company and the product (the cream cheese) and toward the customer (how the cream cheese fits into her life, along with everything else). You can't do that if you don't have this sort of context.

EXERCISE

CREATING CONTEXT

Make a list of the brand-name products you use every day—deodorant, shampoo, cereal, peanut butter, candy, what have you. With each product, write down a short description of how you use it.

Next, draw a chart like the one here, with at least four concentric squares. Choose one of the products from your list and write its best quality in the center square.

EXERCISE

CREATING CONTEXT *(Continued)*

Here's the fun part: In the next larger box, write what's happening that's relevant when you use the product. Then, in the next larger box, widen the aperture a bit and write down more of the context. Keep doing this until you get to the big picture.

Finally, compare this complex chart with just the "how" part. See the difference? One narrows the inquiry, and the other provides any number of options for creative marketing. One is convergent, and the other is divergent. One is logic; the other is energy.

SPELL IT OUT

Along with finding the context comes making it clear. Most consumer interviewers are fairly empathetic and intuitive, and can understand what's implied in the responses they get. But the nuances and energy are often difficult to transmit to others, and my clients may miss some important details. For their benefit, I ask the consumers to spell out for me all the implications and correlations in whatever situation we're discussing. I ask them to imagine that I'm from Mars and to explain the situation to me as if I've never seen or done whatever is involved myself.

What exactly is going on here? If things are spelled out in a very literal and specific way, it's much easier to fully appreciate the information. And when I ask people to spell things out for me, I also find that some of my assumptions weren't exactly on target, either. When your respondents expand their responses beyond a monosyllabic answer, you'll find that you gain a much broader, richer, deeper understanding.

UNDERNEATH THE CHOP

For me, the process of asking questions is akin to my experience as a scuba diver. On the surface of the ocean, there's always this kind of superficial, chattery chop. But once you dive in and pull yourself down the anchor line, you get underneath that chop, and you discover an amazing world down there.

This is what I always think about when I'm interviewing people: I need to find ways to get underneath that surface chop and down to that really cool world where there are a lot of currents and undertows and lovely coral that blooms at night and parrot fish. It's fascinating once you're there—you lose all your self-consciousness because what's going on around you is so amazing.

IMAGINING THE IDEAL

All the exercises that I use when I'm interviewing people—"imagine this, imagine that, draw this, picture that"—are simply ways to get people to give me some indication of what their ideal would be.

I'll say to people, "Oh, the real reason we're here is, I'm a wealthy venture capitalist, and I'm going to start my ideal fill-in-the-blank company." I'm always intrigued by the results I get when people start thinking about what the ideal might be (rather than simply responding to what already exists).

I did this with my students at Northwestern University. I asked them, what would be the ideal food company for grad students at Northwestern? Right now, either they're captive to what's in the vending machine in the basement or they have to walk 10 minutes to go to the student center, where the people are rude, the food is greasy, and the lines are long.

They said, "Well . . . the food would be fresh." "It would be convenient." "It would come to us." Then one student said, "It would be on wheels." Remember the technique of listening for energy? This was the comment that got the discussion crackling.

So then we started thinking about what's on wheels, and the image that evolved was a cart, like a tea cart. Somebody would come at class break times, every hour on the hour, and there would be smoothies and bagels and sandwiches and salads and fruit and baby carrots and every kind of healthy stuff. That was their ideal.

And then I had them talk about the current reality—what's really here? Well, it's greasy food and long lines in a dingy and noisy place with rude employees who don't listen and turn their back on you, or else it's packaged cookies and candy bars in the basement.

Judging from the excitement and energy in the room while the students brainstormed about their ideal company, there's a huge business opportunity waiting for someone to take advantage of it. Maybe some of my students will; who knows?

CREATING AND USING EXERCISES

Sometimes, just sitting and asking questions isn't enough to get you underneath the chop to the ocean floor. On the following pages are some very powerful exercises that you can use to help you get at what's down there.

And because it's very important that you be familiar with these techniques before you use them, so that you can "sell" people on them with confidence, there are instructions for how you can practice them on yourself and with a few helpful volunteers.

A COAT OF ARMS

I ask people I'm interviewing to draw a shield on a piece of paper—a typical knight's shield, with a swoopy top and a heart-shaped bottom. I then ask them to divide it into four quadrants and draw something in each one of them, just like a coat of arms for a royal family.

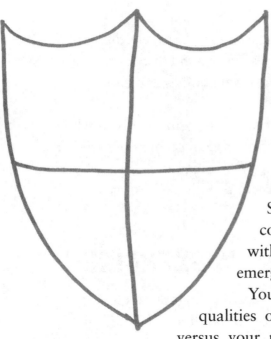

They draw things that represent the qualities they think a particular brand has—anything that would symbolize those qualities. Imagine the difference between a coat of arms for Old Spice, say, and one for Secret. Or between a coat of arms for Black & Decker and one for Sears. The nonlinear, emotional connections that people have with a particular brand often emerge on a coat of arms.

You can do this to imagine the qualities or activities of your ideal day versus your real days. The dis-coherencies are where the untapped energy lies.

EXERCISE

COAT OF ARMS ANALYSIS

Using the outline of the shield on the previous page, draw two coats of arms, each representing a different brand of the same type of product.

When you're done, without showing them yours, have two friends or coworkers perform the same exercise for the same products.

Then sit down with the two of them and discuss the results. Try to interpret their drawings before they explain them to you. Ask for confirmation. Listen for the energy and context in their replies.

This is a way of getting your intuitive/emotional right brain to comprehend the brand's personality. When you understand the product with both the intuitive and the logical sides of your brain, you have a better chance of making discoveries about it—such as what draws people to one brand rather than another.

BEFORE, DURING, AND AFTER: THE THREE-PANEL CARTOON

I'll have people draw a three-panel cartoon: They draw themselves before, during, and after an experience. They write their spoken conversations and a thought bubble of what's going through their minds, and they put a title on the bottom of each panel.

For instance, instead of saying to a 55-year-old man, "Tell me about buying insurance for your family," and having him respond, "Well, I meet with the guy, and then I make a decision, and blah blah blah," I have him draw a before-during-after cartoon. In the middle panel, the "during," what's coming out of the salesperson's mouth is all hieroglyphics, and the thought bubble by the guy's head is, "Holy smokes, what's he talking about?"

In a traditional interview, would he ever tell me that?

In an interview about snack foods, I had a woman do this same three-panel cartoon exercise. In the first frame, she was sitting at her computer, thinking, "I really shouldn't, oh maybe I will, what the heck."

In the middle one, she was on a beach, on a 30-second vacation.

In the "after" panel, she drew what she called the "Rain of Guilt," and it was as if she were in the middle of a cyclone.

The power of the image was intense. It's one thing to tell somebody, "Oh, yes, people feel guilty after snacking." But, when you look at the picture, filled with remorse and angst and all the ways she hates herself, you truly understand the emotion going on there and the level of intense energy that is just ripe to be tapped.

APTER

"Rain of Guilt"

EXERCISE

THREE-PANEL CARTOONING

Pick one of the earlier exercises in this book (and I know you've done them all!), preferably the one that made you the most uncomfortable, and draw a before-during-after cartoon that describes the process of completing that exercise. Remember, give each panel a title and show your thought bubbles.

Next, ask a friend or coworker to draw a three-panel cartoon about another life experience: proposing marriage, giving birth, eating a new brand of cereal, or whatever.

Look for ideas that that person normally would not have expressed aloud. Again, we're accessing the right-brain emotional side and doing an end run around the logical, analytical, self-editing habits of the left brain. When you discover "secrets" (like the Rain of Guilt), you have raw creative material that can be used in any number of ways. You're hunting for the unexpected, for the flash of insight.

A PATH THROUGH THE DAY

Sometimes I have people draw me a path through their day, from the time they wake up in the morning until they go to sleep at night. I ask them to show me their basic activities—how they spend major chunks of their time during a typical day.

They draw little stick figures: here I am eating breakfast, here I am going to work, here I am at work at my little stick-figure computer, here I am eating lunch, here's my cigarette break.

Then, if I'm working with snack users, for example, I ask them to draw in where they had a snack and how it changed the path of their day. You could see the particular pattern that emerged: People were carving out momentary oases in a busy day, retreating from the usual path of routine. This is a great exercise for any regular habit or product use that you want to explore, and the actual moment of the activity can be further illuminated if necessary by using a three-panel cartoon.

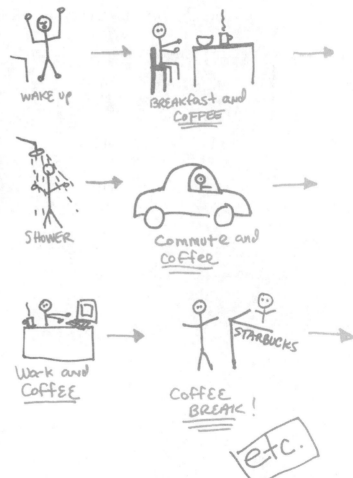

EXERCISE

MAPPING THE PATH

You guessed it! Based on this example, it's time to have someone draw a map through his or her day. Decide in advance what behavior you want to look for, and ask the person to include it: coffee or soda drinking, gum chewing, snack eating, and so on. What insight do you get into this person's habits and life? What surprises you?

THE INTERNAL WEATHER REPORT

When my son was little, I tried to teach him how to talk about his emotions, which is a hard thing to do. When my older daughter was young, she would tell me everything: "Hmm, I was feeling a little grumpy earlier today, but now I'm more calm," but my son would answer in single syllables.

"How ya doing?"

"Fine."

"Fine? That's it? Just fine?"

"Fine."

So I'd ask, what's the internal weather report? Is it sunny, is it cloudy, is it lightning bolts, is it a cyclone, is it a hurricane? What's happening on the inside?

These days, I'll tell the story about how I got my little boy to talk about his feelings, and then I'll have people draw their internal weather report, using the weather symbols. I ask them to add these symbols to the path through their day (previous exercise).

I did this on a few occasions with teenage girls. You always hear that their peers are really important to them, but this exercise really illustrated the depth of that feeling.

I had them draw a path through their day, noting especially when they spent time with their friends. Then, at each activity, I had them draw in a tiny internal weather report. The only time there were little sunshine icons was in the moments in the hall between classes when they were with their friends and after school when they were with their friends. At night, when it was time to go to bed, one girl drew rain because she was sad that she wouldn't see her friends for another eight hours.

How does all this connect with creativity? All of these exercises bring you a greater and clearer understanding of someone else's mind and point of view. You become their advocate. You think, "If I were in this person's place, what would I want and need?" The more you can humanize and add dimension to the people you're talking to, the more real they become.

We're good at reducing people to numbers ("Tweens drive up to X-Y% of family purchases!"), but not so good at understanding the real emotions that drive people. Marketing based on numbers feels logical–analytical–left brain. When you're truly in touch with the people you're trying to communicate with, you're accessing that emotional-intuitive side, the side that can't be analyzed.

EXERCISE

DRAWING THE INTERNAL WEATHER REPORT

The internal weather report is another great tool. Have the friend who helped you with the previous exercise pencil in the weather icons for each activity on his or her path through the day.

For extra credit, you may have the person do a three-panel cartoon for each time he or she engages in the activity you're measuring.

Put it all together, and what have you got? Certainly a lot more than you would have if you'd sat the person down and asked, "Tell me about your experience with your breakfast cereal."

FROM CFOs TO 12-YEAR-OLDS

When I began doing this kind of work, I wasn't sure what response I would get to these kinds of exercises. Would drawing a cartoon be too "out there" for people to really engage in? Who is really going to draw me an "internal weather report" and take it seriously?

Well, everyone.

Interestingly, when I present these exercises in a matter-of-fact way, I find that people just dive in and do them, whether I have an audience of CFOs or of 12-year-old girls. That broad willingness to respond just proves the effectiveness of having an open and curious attitude. The process is about the person you're questioning, not about you. You hold the space, you introduce the questions and the exercises, but it's the people you're listening to who take you below the chop, who reveal what's in the world below the surface.

I invite you to share the dis-coherencies you uncover with us on our Web site, www.energyinfuser.com. We'll create a virtual "warehouse" of these dis-coherencies, and if you're ever stuck for an idea, you can visit the site, pick up a couple of ripe dis-coherencies, and use them as the source of natural idea-creating energy.

It becomes your task, then, to listen for the energy, to look for associations, to find connections that other people might not have made before. By doing this, you can proceed to the next step: releasing potential energy.

4 RELEASING POTENTIAL ENERGY

Every situation in our lives has some sort of potential energy that is waiting to be discovered and tapped into. This can take the form of tension or unresolved conflict: "I want this, but I also want that." Merely focusing on the "this" or the "that" does not make for very exciting possibilities. But discovering and releasing that potential energy can lead to some very high-voltage results indeed. This chapter is about finding the hidden conflicts that motivate us all.

In physics, "potential energy" is stored energy, energy that is waiting to be released. A tensely coiled spring is just waiting to explode outward and transform its potential energy into kinetic energy.

We all innately long for the resolution of tension. Seeing a coiled spring, you know that it will eventually burst forth; in a suspenseful movie, you know in a quiet

$$PE_s = \tfrac{1}{2}Kx^2$$

$$PE_g = mgh$$

$$PE_k = \tfrac{1}{2}mv^2$$

$$PE_v = gED$$

scene that something or someone will pop out and scare the life out of you; the last chords of a symphony lead inevitably to the tonic chord, to provide a satisfying conclusion. (Try singing "shave and a haircut" without topping it off with "—two bits." Leaving the musical phrase hanging unresolved is almost painful.)

Malachy Walsh, my mentor and friend, teaches that the energy arising from tension is the force that moves society forward. All of us have needs, appetites, duties, and responsibilities that drive us through each day—from short-range issues ("What will I have for lunch?") to long-range ones ("How can I make my family's life better?"). These needs often pull us in a number of directions at once: I want to buy groceries for my family according to my own personal standards, and yet I'd like someone else to do the grunt work so that I can spend my time elsewhere. It seems that you can't have it both ways—you have to either invest a substantial amount of time in grocery expeditions or turn over the responsibility to someone else and take the risk that the task won't be completed in a way that satisfies you.

We'll come back to the idea of potential energy and how to release it, but first, let's take a broader view. You'll see how Thomas Edison's "turn it upside down" motto applies to the world of brand development.

NEW AND IMPROVED

In the olden days, innovations that filled consumers' unmet functional needs were enough to build a major brand. Floor wax that dissolved the old wax and applied the new in one step, for example. Shampoo and conditioner with vitamins to make your hair shiny and strong. Paper towels that soaked up spills faster than the competition. But in today's marketplace, most of those important needs are already filled by a brand, and usually by more than one.

We have a huge proliferation of choices in every category. When I took my adolescent son shopping for deodorant for the first time, his eyes bugged out of his head when he looked at the hundreds of choices. Antiperspirant? Deodorant? Roll-on or gel or stick? Which scent? Which brand? In the end, he'll choose the brand that his class mates say is cool. Or the one that has the funny ad on MTV and the graphics that grab him.

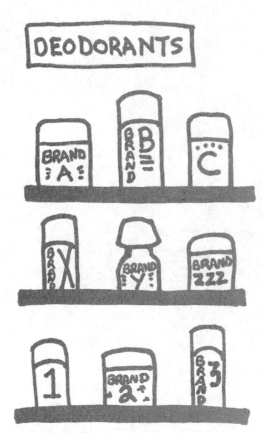

Unfortunately, the brand teams that create those products focus the majority of their innovative efforts on creating superior formulations for their products.

What they don't realize is, their target audience is looking for that and for something more.

EXERCISE

WHY DO YOU BUY WHAT YOU BUY?— PART ONE

Take out your last grocery list or receipt and write down all the brand-name items you purchased. Then do the same with the last brand-name products you picked up at the mall.

EXERCISE

WHY DO YOU BUY WHAT YOU BUY?— PART ONE (Continued)

What made you buy what you bought, compared to the alternatives that you could have bought?

What was it about that brand of juice, that style of sneakers, those headphones, that kind of perfume or cologne?

How much of your selection had to do with a formulation or some technical feature or a discount price, and how much had to do with an image or an idea?

Sometimes the rational reason is the intellectual alibi for the emotional satisfaction. Pick one of the products you bought and imagine: If that brand were a world, what would that world be like? Where would it be located? What time of day would it be? Who would inhabit it? Then ask yourself, is that world a place you'd like to live? To visit? If so, maybe there's more to your brand choice than meets the eye.

What's Going On Here ¿

Everyone selects the products he buys for different reasons, but it's interesting to note what those reasons are, when there is so much to choose from . . . especially if cost is not a factor.

In the marketing of products, it's easy to forget that consumers are more interested in how a product makes them feel than in what a product does (and how it does it).

BRAND FIRST, PRODUCT SECOND

Grown-ups tend to sort things first by product class and then by brand. In other words, when we need new sneakers, we look for cross-trainers first, then we look at brands and offerings within that category. By contrast, kids today seem to sort these choices by brand first, and then product. So they'll choose the Adidas brand first, then look for the type of product they need.

I first noticed this profound shift while I was doing focus groups for a confection company. First I interviewed grown-ups, and then I interviewed teenagers. I asked both groups to draw how they imagined two worlds; the first was the world of sugar candy, and the second was the world of chocolate candy. The grown-ups drew worlds with recognizable candy shapes—licorice twists for the supports for a swing set, lollipops for trees. The teenagers drew brands—Twizzlers for the swing-set supports, Twix for the couch, Rollos for the tree trunks, and Fruit by the Foot for the tree leaves. Each group had a different orientation.

We are moving toward a population of consumers who process the world primarily in terms of a brand's voice, personality, and world. Rational, tangible product attributes are still important, but less as a way of distinguishing one brand from another; instead, they are important in terms of how they bring a brand's world to life.

Marketers whose products succeed create innovative brand worlds first, then deliver those innovative brand worlds with new, tangible product attributes that pay off the brand imagery. Those tangible attributes might be packaging, fragrance, or distribution—not the traditional kind of innovation that's initially dreamed up by R&D during the product's formulation.

THE TRADITIONAL INNOVATION PROCESS

Traditionally, product innovations came from R&D people, who made interesting new formulations aimed at filling important and unmet needs in a category.

Then the marketing department would describe those product features by writing a sentence or two about each and printing that information on a card. The marketing research people would bring a bunch of those cards to consumers and record which features they liked the most and which they said they would be most likely to buy.

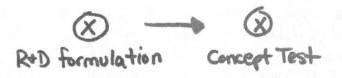

Finally, the marketing people would take the winning concept and give it to the ad agency, which would figure out the appropriate brand voice, personality, and world.

The problem with this process is that in today's marketplace, it is inadequate to the task. It generates ideas that consumers will say are "great for camping"—in other words, things that seem clever but are not really relevant to everyday life (which is the Kiss of Death Assessment for any new idea).

In today's marketplace, where there are literally dozens of kinds of OJ to choose from, a product innovation that begins in the lab is unlikely to make enough of a difference to succeed. Back to my son in the drugstore eyeing the deodorant choices. A fancy new formula that keeps him 20 percent drier just isn't going to be enough to get him. Something that's cool, a brand name that conjures up an attitude he aspires to, a graphic that evokes a world of imagery that captures his imagination . . . those things will be. Of course, the product has to work, too. Image alone is also not enough.

A NEW INNOVATION PROCESS

Because today's consumers are moved by a brand's voice, personality, and world as much as they are by specific product features, the innovation process must begin with the end in mind. We begin by assessing what brand imagery is missing from a category, then we drill down and ideate tangible product features that bring that imagery to life, and then we hand that information to R&D so that it can make prototypes. We've set the traditional process on its head.

But how do you know where exactly to begin? This is trickier than it sounds. In order to work, the imagery needs to resonate with consumers. It needs to touch them in a way that is meaningful to them and in a way that is fresh and interesting.

The key here is to tap into the potential energy of a situation. That energy comes from the tension created by the conflicts—the paradoxes—that are part of everyone's daily life.

OH, WELL

These consumer paradoxes tug at us every day, so often that we don't even consciously notice them. Every decision we come to, every action we take, requires a trade-off. We spend our mental energy sorting through alternatives, doing "lesser-of-two-evils" balancing. Most paradoxical situations are shrugged off with "oh, well"—that's the way it is; life isn't perfect; you can't always get what you want. Mostly, we choose to complain rather than create.

> The vending machines on campus stock only candy and chips, but what the students need and want are fresh fruits and veggies and low-cal protein. Oh, well.
> Babies scream on airplanes when business travelers want peace. Oh, well.
> A challenging career demands the investment of time, as does a satisfying home and family life. Oh, well.

Paradox exists at many levels, from the product-focused ("I want a shiny, waxed floor, but I don't want to spend the time and energy to remove the old wax first") to the spiritual/psychological ("I want to be passively entertained, and I want to be spiritually nourished"—thank you, Oprah Winfrey).

In other words, it is the intersection of needs that creates potential energy and the possibility of creating an interesting resolution to a problem. If you simply identify a need as a flat statement ("People want to be healthy")—well, that leaves a thousand directions open and has little energy. There is no particular option to home in on, and there is not enough grist for the idea mill.

However, if you think of the issue as "People want to be healthy, but they don't want to change any of their habits," that ripens and focuses the challenge. If you imagine these desires as arrows moving perpendicular to each other, the point of intersection is where the potential energy lies. Starting there, you can begin thinking of a solution that solves the problem in each direction.

People want to
be healthy ⟶ ✳ Ideas

People don't want
to make an
extraordinary effort

Consumers are dealing with perpendicular arrows in every area of life—holding onto conflicting desires or expectations or demands simultaneously. Products that make a real impact on the marketplace don't just resolve tensions and conflicts, they resolve those tensions and conflicts in a unique way. A high-voltage idea releases the potential energy, and there are sparks, light, and heat.

ACKNOWLEDGE THE CONFLICT

Instead of trying to ignore the conflicting desires in a situation, successful brands acknowledge the paradox and resolve it in a fresh and interesting way.

Target: I want to be stylish and hip, but I don't want to spend a lot of money.

Before Target reinvigorated its image, shopping at a discount retailer wasn't something to be ashamed of, perhaps, but it certainly wasn't anything to draw attention to. Many stores radiated an air of "you don't want to be here, and we don't either, but at least you're saving a couple of bucks." Target identified this conflict and removed the inferiority complex from its stores and its product lines.

Nike: Participating in sports is exhilarating, but I'm out of shape and tired, so I'll watch somebody else do it on TV.

Nike has taken on the challenge of making the difficulty of exercise its selling point: "Just do it," even though it's tough.

EXERCISE

CREATIVITY FROM CONFLICT

For each of the following conflicts, come up with a high-voltage idea for a product or service that resolves the conflict in a unique way.

"I want to be happy and comfortable in my home, but I'm very concerned about the environmental effects of manufacturing and using certain products."

"I want to be able to enjoy popular culture with my children, but I'm afraid of exposing them to violent images."

"I want to do work away from the office, but I don't want to sit home all day, either."

"I want to start my own business, but I don't have enough money to hire a support staff."

"I want to be able to eat at restaurants with my friends, but I'm limited by my dietary restrictions."

For more dis-coherencies or to add yours, visit our Web site at www.energyinfuser.com.

AGAIN: LOGIC VERSUS ENERGY

A single product can address more than one conflict. For example, a consumer who is shopping for skin-care products is unconsciously trying to resolve paradoxes such as:

I want it fast, but I want it to be exactly right for me.
I want to be in control, even when someone else is the expert.
I love my best self, but I'm afraid it's not enough.

The common element in these paradoxes is that they are emotional; they deal with our vulnerabilities and anxieties. As we go through the day, we make choices based on instincts and feelings that we may barely understand; we aren't aware of these paradoxes on a conscious level, but they still hold us in their grip.

Again, this harks back to listening for logic versus listening for energy. Logic dictates that consumers will always buy the most efficient product—the product that is the most nutritious, that cleans windows without streaking, that gets the best gas mileage. All things being equal, they will purchase the least expensive alternative.

But of course, transactions (dynamic ones) aren't based only on logical reasons. If they were, we'd all make our coffee at home, we'd wear sensible shoes, and the generic black-and-white-label brands from the 1970s would be the only things sold on supermarket shelves.

A successful product has something more, something that satisfies a buyer emotionally, fulfilling more than one need. The consumer won't necessarily be able to put her finger on just what led her to make her choice, but the magnetic attraction is there just the same.

EXERCISE

WHY DO YOU BUY WHAT YOU BUY?— PART TWO

Return to the first part of this exercise and look at your list of explanations for buying the products you bought.

Now that you know more about the magnetic attraction of potential energy, zero in on some of your favorite purchases and identify the internal conflicts and paradoxes that each of these products addressed for you.

CLIMBING DOWN
THE BENEFIT LADDER

Let's take a step back to the traditional way of doing things.

A "benefit ladder" is a diagram of the ordinary innovation process, beginning with the new formulation that R&D came up with and connecting it with the benefit to consumers. Benefit ladders were considered to be innovative 20-odd years ago, but they have led us to a point where we're grasping at straws to give brands an impact.

If you've never seen one, a benefit ladder is a diagram with three boxes, with arrows leading up from the bottom to the top. The idea is that you begin with the product in the bottom box, move up to the immediate, tangible benefit in the next box ("tastes great" or "more absorbent" or "less mess"), and then move up to a broader emotional benefit in the top box. Unfortunately, the top box always seemed to be "be a better mom," "achieve world peace," or "have better (or more) sex."

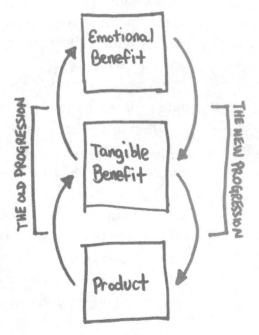

Well, so far, I've managed to keep my kids in one piece as I've raised them, and which brand of paper towels I used doesn't seem to have mattered. The rungs at the top of the benefit ladder don't seem to be connected to the others, at least when you're climbing up from below. Getting to the top rung is a real stretch.

I have advised my clients to think about climbing downward. In the top box, put a consumer conflict that needs resolution: "I want to have a clean house, but cleaning is a pain in the neck, it's messy, and it's no fun." Then think about what is going to resolve this tension—what tangible attributes can a product have that address this conflict in more than one direction, in a fresh way? Then you move to the bottom box, and voilà, you have Swiffer, or Scrubbing Bubbles, or a wind-tunnel vacuum cleaner.

"OF COURSE!"

Products that identify a conflict, resolve it, and thus release potential energy successfully often have a feel of inevitability about them; they are ideas that make you think, "Of course!" It's not until the answer appears that the question seems obvious. Sometimes the product is an advance in technology, like the cell phone. Other times, it's merely a new combination of existing technology.

"Swiping your credit card right at the gas pump? Why didn't someone think of this before?"

Of course, being ahead of the curve technologically is no guarantee of success. The Apple Newton didn't catch on, but the Palm Pilot became ubiquitous. It's all about striking the societal psyche at the right moment.

Once, the idea that people would pay for water seemed absurd; enter the fitness boom and concerns about municipal water. Before the ascendancy of Starbucks, a four-dollar cup of coffee was a ridiculous notion. When ATMs were introduced, the prevailing wisdom said that people wouldn't trust a machine to do their banking.

EXERCISE

FINDING THE INSPIRATION

Identify the resolved conflict in the following "of course!" offerings. Then go to the mall and find at least 10 products or stores that give you a similar feeling.

Sony Walkman
Cinnabon
TiVo digital video recorder
Birkenstock sandals
The Body Shop
Amazon.com
Gladware disposable containers
Apple iPod

JUST ADD WATER

When you've climbed down the ladder from consumer conflict to tangible benefit, the goal is to clearly make the connection between the product and the emotional conflict it resolves. Think about Kraft's Easy Mac. This kid-targeted version of good old macaroni and cheese wasn't sold on its "just add water" premise. The commercials showed kids at home in the afternoon, making a snack for themselves and bickering as siblings do. Mom wasn't around—most likely, she was at work. This wasn't a fantasy vision of a perfect family; it was closer to a picture of how Mom hopes her kids are getting along before she gets home (able to work a microwave and get a decent snack). We weren't hit over the head with it . . . it wasn't even stated at all. The dialogue of the commercial was the smart-alecky younger sister bothering her brother as he made the Easy Mac. But it was a picture of life that was instantly understood by millions of women (and men): I want my kids to have something decent to eat, but I can't be there to make it for them.

EASE OF PREPARATION **VS.** EASE OF MIND

IDENTIFYING PARADOX

To get you attuned to looking for kinetic conflict and sources of potential energy, let's consider a couple of examples.

If our target consumers are women entering midlife, the conflict might be:

Just as my inner self is becoming visible, my outer self renders me invisible.

As a woman is leaving the intensive years of child rearing and is finally done with dirty diapers and trips to the baseball field, she is coming into herself. Perhaps she is getting to pursue her own interests—writing her own poetry, becoming a Pilates instructor, spending more time on herself in any number of ways. At the same time, when she walks down a street, where she used to garner a fair amount of attention (if only from appreciative construction workers), she now passes unnoticed. When she goes into a clothing store, the saleswomen flock to her teenage daughter and ignore her completely.

In my approach, the first step is to create boards filled with images that bring each side of the conflict to life. (See Chapter 5.) Then we gather things from different categories that resolve that paradox. In this case, it might be pictures of Susan Sarandon, Madonna, a Wonderbra, and a self-published volume of poetry. Our work is to translate their features into our client's category.

Stand back and look at elements that might cross over to whatever you're trying to develop, whether it be a hair-care product or a fast-food dinner. What could you adopt? What's inspiring? What's grist for the mill?

Let's consider another consumer group: 10- to 12-year-old boys. I know this group well, as I live with one of these delightful creatures. A conflict for this group might be:

Treat me like a grown-up, but tuck me in at night.

My son wants to be grown up: He has a phone extension in his room, but if a call comes after nine-thirty, which is his bedtime, I am supposed to say that he's "not available," rather than that he's "in bed").

He goes to Starbucks, but he orders hot chocolate (or sometimes coffee with five sugars and a gallon of milk).

He still has his teddy bear, but Mr. Bear has a special bed in the closet.

He's slowly making the transition from one stage to the next, wanting the grown-up things but not wanting to let go of the boy things yet.

In addition, he's going through all the bodily changes that boys his age go through, so add an extra level of anxiety on top of everything else. He and his peers deal with the tension by making fun of it—witness the success of the "Grossology" exhibit that toured science museums across the country, delving into the science behind every bodily function and excretion you'd ever (or never) want to know about.

So, what things resolve these conflicts? Gap Kids and Abercrombie (the younger version of Abercrombie & Fitch) provide smaller-size versions of hip grown-up clothes. Computer games touch on this tension as well—it's still playing games, but with high-level technology.

But what about the bodily changes aspect of the situation? Again, think back to my son staring at the hundreds of choices of deodorant on the shelf. If we were developing a deodorant for this age group, we'd look at the perpendicular arrows of "I want to have what the adults have, but made for me" and "I'm grossed out by what's happening to my body, but I can make fun of it."

At the point where those arrows collide and the potential energy lies, you'd be likely to find something like a smaller version of Arrid Extra Dry or Right Guard, with a Sweat-ology game that you could download from the Web site and play.

IT ALL BOILS DOWN TO THIS

ADAPT TO THE CONSUMER

Whether you're looking at women in midlife, boys in adolescence, or anyone else, the thing to remember about potential energy is that it lies within conflicts of consumer desire: The product adapts to the consumer, not the other way around. To truly understand the paradoxes that pull at someone, it's necessary to step further into that person's world, to make the Copernican Shift.

 # OPEN THE APERTURE

Who is your target audience? What do you know about those people? Most marketing efforts include consumer research, but too often that research provides a narrow, limited view of consumers, seeing them only as consumers rather than as three-dimensional human beings. By "opening the aperture" and taking a broader view of the people you're trying to reach, with a fuller sense of who they are, you can transform the way you approach your marketing.

"So, tell me," I begin, looking at the eight people gathered around the overpolished conference table, blinking in the fluorescent lights. The group has been selected because they all have something in common: They are all devoted users of my client's product. They've come here to share their insight, to give me the insider's view on—

"Cream cheese. Let's talk about cream cheese. Now, how exactly do you go about spreading cream cheese on your bagel? Let's start with this end of the table . . . "

Absurd? Absolutely. Yet serious, intense discussions of how exactly you spread cream cheese—or squeeze toothpaste, or sprinkle carpet deodorizer—go on every day.

Everyone knows that businesses are supposed to do consumer-led research, but in fact they look at people through a narrow perspective: How do they interact with My Product? We know these people only in terms of their behavior within a category: We know them as heavy users of cotton balls or car wax. This (naturally) provides you with only a tiny piece of who these people are—it doesn't give you enough juice to understand how to reinvent the whole brand.

When there is only narrow research and understanding, the brand itself appears narrow. You have to widen the aperture, to see the user in a broader context. Brands that do this take on a fuller dimension themselves. Take a look at Ben & Jerry's—it assumes that its consumers care about other things besides ice cream. The VW Bug has a sense of wit about it—it was designed to evoke a smile, not just mimic every other streamlined box on wheels.

How do you go about opening your aperture and seeing the consumer in a fuller way? First, you need to make the Copernican Shift in your point of view.

THE COPERNICAN SHIFT

In 1530, the astronomer Nicolas Copernicus published his work *De Revolutionibus*, which asserted that, contrary to popular belief, the earth was not the center of the universe. Keep in mind that all his observations were made with the naked eye—this was a hundred years before the invention of the telescope. Copernicus's idea was violently rejected by scientists and religious authorities alike, and definitive proof of it did not come along for 150 years. But even before supporting evidence was gathered, forward thinkers had already adopted this new paradigm: Man was not smugly placed in the center of everything, but rather was clinging to one small sphere in a vast universe. This change in paradigm—what I call the Copernican Shift—was an important step in the maturation of science; astronomers would no longer be content to accept what appeared to be obvious.

When you are looking at any problem situation, keep Copernicus in mind. What assumptions are you making? Are you (and your product) in the center of the universe? Really?

EXERCISE

YOUR OWN COPERNICAN SHIFT— PART ONE

The Copernican Shift is a powerful tool for positive transformation, for the marketing of a product, or even for yourself. Do this exercise before you begin reading the rest of this chapter.

On the next page, draw a circle with the name of your company, product, or service, or even your own name, in the center.

In orbit around it, write the names of the different critical factors that the company, product, or service (or you) interacts with. You can model this on the pre-Copernican worldview on the previous page.

For example, if you write a company's name in the center, the orbiting objects could possibly be competitors, employees, customers, Wall Street, and so on. If you write your own name, the orbiting objects could be your spouse, your children, your friends, your career, and your volunteer organization.

You'll find the second part of this exercise later in the chapter.

EXERCISE

YOUR OWN COPERNICAN SHIFT—
PART ONE (Continued)

A NO-NONSENSE APPROACH

I was the director in charge of the No Nonsense Pantyhose account at a leading ad agency in Chicago. Sales were declining, and we were in danger of losing the business. It wasn't that women weren't buying pantyhose; in fact, as greater numbers of women took on careers, they were actually buying more, as wearing pantyhose was required in many offices and businesses.

L'eggs had come out with its cute packaging and sexy advertising using the rock tune "She's Got Legs," by ZZ Top. Its support hose were called "Sheer Energy," while No Nonsense's were called "Light Support." No Nonsense was seen as being just that: down-to-earth, pragmatic, and not very sexy.

The team went and looked at the research for clues. Like Freud, we wondered: What did women want? More specifically, what did they want in a pair of pantyhose? Durability was a key answer, as well as making legs look attractive. But there had to be more . . . what was special about No Nonsense pantyhose?

We enthusiastically went on factory tours in North Carolina, searching for answers. We saw the nylon pellets; we learned about denier; we learned about how waistbands were produced and how the pantyhose were finished (boarded or not, pressed or crumpled); we watched the packaging assembly line. Again I looked for clues: What was the magic ingredient? Was there a magic kind of thread or way of melting the nylon or something unique about the knitting machines?

We had done research, of course, but the research that we had gave us only a narrow picture of the women who wore pantyhose. It asked them what they wanted in pantyhose, then asked them to rate different brands of pantyhose against those desirable attributes. Later in the questionnaire, the women's age, income, employment status, marital status, and so on, would be asked for. We never got a picture of the complete woman; we saw her only in relation to what she wore on her legs. But looking at all of the information together, we found that what working women wanted most in their pantyhose was durability (and looks).

This was the Copernican Shift: Instead of looking at women from the perspective of the client, we turned the telescope around and looked at the client from the perspective of the women. What did working women want? What were their lives like? What role did their appearance play in their lives? What role did pantyhose play in their overall appearance—both positively and negatively?

There was the answer. Working women at that time wanted to look put together—color-coordinated and stylish in an appropriate way, a way that would neither attract inappropriate attention nor detract from a professional image. Their jobs were a big part of how they saw themselves, and their physical appearance was an important part of their career success. They might not have been dressed out of the *Dress for Success* manual of the early 1980s, but they were definitely conscious of the impact that their appearance had on their image and their perceived competence. Anything that detracted—poor grooming, a too-revealing outfit, scuffed shoes, tarnished silver jewelry, snagged pantyhose—compromised their polished appearance and the way they felt about their competence.

We started by empathizing with the woman the client was trying to reach. We tried first to see her as a whole person, then to understand how the client's product fit within her world. Using this as the strategy, we wrote ads that portrayed this empathetic understanding of working women—and kept the business.

EXERCISE

NOTICING

Go to the mall or to the grocery store and start noticing the characteristics of, and the marketing for, different products. For each product, ask, Is this product presented as if it were the center of the universe? (In other words, are its features trumpeted more than the benefits it offers? Is the product designed with the user in mind? Is it beautiful or utilitarian?) Or does it seem that the product is presented as fitting in as just one part of the customer's whole life? Make a list of what strikes you about a range of products.

Then leave the store and go to the zoo, or out into nature. Look at the animals and plants. Which of them act as if they were the center of their own universe, and which seem to have adapted to fit in with the grander scheme of things.

Now look at popular entertainment (music, books, television shows, movies), government policies, and even the other people in your life, and evaluate them by the same criteria.

Begin to arrange your lists into groups. What do you notice?

What's Going On Here ¿

What it all comes down to is this: Are the things you encounter inwardly focused or outwardly focused? If they are inwardly focused, they may present themselves as if they were the center of the universe. If they are outwardly focused, they happily coexist in orbit. As you do this exercise, keep this question in mind: Which approach appears to be more successful?

THE ENERGY IS IN THE LISTENER

With many of my clients, the first step I take is to help them understand that they are not seeing the world through their consumers' eyes. They are looking at their consumers rather than experiencing the world as their consumers experience it. The client thinks that the energy is happening within the company or its processes or its packages or its product formulas, but the real energy is happening within its consumers—their lives, their hopes, their families.

Many companies that still see themselves as the center of the universe want to increase their gravitational pull, so to speak, and draw their consumers in closer. A company that has made the Copernican Shift understands that it is a moon circling its consumer—she is the center of her own world. The company can increase the brightness and the clarity with which it shines in the sky, making itself stand out from the starry background, but it isn't at the center of things.

I remember the words of a philosophy instructor I had. He said that the energy in a conversation really happened inside the listener, not inside the speaker. This is exactly what happens with the Copernican Shift—it's where your message lands and what the listener does with it that are really important.

EMPATHY BOARDS

How do you go about making the Copernican Shift and seeing the world from a consumer-centric perspective? To see people in a broader way, you must understand the world they travel through. This is almost the reverse of the "path through the day" exercise—you must follow in a person's footsteps and re-create the world that person sees.

Think about the way the forensic investigators on prime-time detective television shows go about solving the crime: They lay out each piece of the evidence and see what the picture that is created then tells them—which is often different from the hypothesis that they had at the beginning. What you're really doing is forensic reconstruction of a person's daily life.

To really empathize with the people you want to reach, you need to understand the visceral emotion underlying the part of their world that you are exploring. I've conducted groups with people from every age group, diving under the surface to see what drives their world, what fuels their passion.

When I take a group through guided imagery exercises, I've found that it doesn't take long before strong emotional responses pour out from the people in the group, with the intensity of their feelings often surprising them (and me). A woman who was raising three children described how she saw her family literally growing like a garden as she watered and tended it; preteen girls described the gray anxiety and loneliness that they felt between the hours when they saw their friends; and a group of men who were interested in home improvement (normally not the most expressive guys) were overwhelmed with memories of working with their dads when they were young—the smell of sawdust, paint, and glue was still vivid and clear.

Once you've dug your way down to the place where the emotion is glowing like some sort of radioactive ore, how do you maintain the strength and power of that energy?

I like to create collages, or "empathy boards." This is a technique that I use to try to capture the texture of someone's life and experience in a way that can be communicated to someone else visually—a way to try to hang on to the elemental drives that you've uncovered in the people you're trying to reach. It keeps you from getting lost in typical marketing jargon—it keeps the juice in your concept and stops that concept from drying out into something flat and unexciting.

Let's look at an example.

PIECE BY PIECE

What goes into these empathy boards? You want these boards to be teeming with imagery—photographs, drawings, and quotations—that gives context to the life of the person you're trying to understand. What are the conflicts? What things resolve those conflicts?

Think about every step this person takes throughout his or her day. What sorts of things might he or she come in contact with?

Where does he go? What kinds of outdoor spaces does he visit? Urban, rural, or suburban? Gardens? Cityscapes? What kind of indoor spaces? Cluttered? Open? Dull? Overstimulating? What passes in front of his eyes?

What is she reading? Newspapers? Magazines? The back of a cereal box? The latest Harry Potter?

What technology or machines does she interact with every day? Video games? Cell phones? Tools? Kitchen appliances? A car? A scooter? A Palm Pilot? A computer?

Who else inhabits his world? Parents? A spouse or life partner? Friends?

Think of the empathy board as a "flash-forward" montage through the day, a series of snapshots of the places and things surrounding the path this person takes every day. What are the dimensions of her world?

It's important that you reach into as many different disciplines as you can think of to find inspirational images. What inspiration can you find in the arts: architecture, painting, drawing, sculpture, folk art, photography?

Look for imagery in the sciences: botany, zoology, archaeology, paleontology, mathematics, physics, chemistry, astronomy.

Looking at Brancusi sculptures or at the graph of an algebraic equation isn't the obvious answer when you're thinking about how to reach, say, college-age boys or over-40 executive women. Answers may not always leap out instantly, but the technique of forcing connections between seemingly unrelated things can give rise to some surprising and unique ideas.

We will explore this and other idea-generating techniques further in the next chapter, "Break the Board."

EXERCISE

YOUR OWN COPERNICAN SHIFT— PART TWO

Earlier in the chapter, you drew your company, your product, your service, or yourself in the center of the universe.

Now it's time to make your own Copernican Shift.

In the center of the universe, write or draw the name of a person or group of people that you're trying to connect with, either interpersonally or through a company, product, or service.

Then put yourself in the place of that person or group. Draw in the orbits of the things you imagine that he, she, or they have to deal with on a regular basis. Put in everything you can think of—and don't forget to put yourself in there.

When you're done, study the drawing and imagine how you relate to the center of this particular universe—and to everything else that's in orbit around it.

6 BREAK THE BOARD

Once you've collected the raw material for your empathy board, what's next? This chapter is about solving problems by making the shift from left- to right-brain thinking. We break loose from the chains of the literal and let our minds function on a new level. Here is where the high-voltage idea is born. The theme of this book has been that creativity is a skill like any other. It can be taught. Are you ready to learn?

We've come quite a way on our journey. We've discussed how to overcome the enemies of ideas, how to ask questions, ways to tap into the potential energy in a situation, and the power of making the Copernican Shift in your point of view.

Now it's time to have some new ideas.

After all the assessments have been made, the situation analyzed, and the conflicts understood, it's time to go into a brainstorming session and see what innovations you can create.

I have some exercises that I use over and over again in ideation sessions. I never know going in just what exactly is going to emerge, but something always does. These exercises are extensions of those that I've presented in earlier chapters, but this time, you have to focus on your own product or situation.

A reminder to those who remain convinced that they're better at analyzing and number crunching than at thinking up new things: This process is a skill that can be developed like any other. To use a classic metaphor, when you first climb onto a bicycle, you have to consciously shift your weight and learn to refine your sense of balance. Soon, it's second nature—then you can move on to scooters, unicycles, Rollerblades, and leaping the Grand Canyon on a motorbike.

And for those of you who come up with piles of new ideas every day, these exercises can help refresh you when you start thinking, "The well is dry—I don't have a fresh idea left in me anywhere."

Rather than just offering a list of exercises, I also want to discuss why and how these techniques can help to change the way you think and conceptualize. This is similar to the "Asking Questions" chapter: It's as important to think about how to be as it is to think about what to do. Understanding the underlying theory can help you approach any problem in a more creative way.

PERSONALITY AND SPIRIT

The theory that I use is based on a model of personality that I learned in executive coaching training. Our personalities have three basic components: our language, our emotions, and our bodies. They intersect with one another like this:

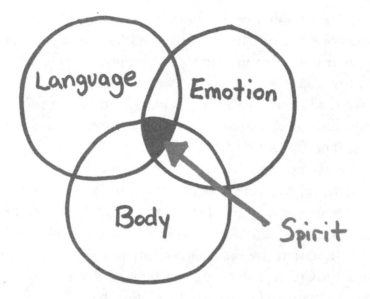

If someone has a personality characteristic, it shows up in each domain. This is a coherency—a way in which a particular trait manifests itself in physicality, language, and emotion.

For instance, if a person is outgoing and friendly in personality, you would expect her to have a relaxed stance, a friendly way of speaking ("Hey! How's it going? How can I be helpful to you? What are you doing this weekend?"), and an upbeat emotional state. If, however, the person has the proverbial "chip on his shoulder," you'd expect his chin to jut out, his conversational tone to be challenging, and his emotional state to be angry and turbulent. Think of someone who is arrogant, someone who is kind, someone who is diligent. You would expect these traits to be reflected in each domain.

In order to grow, a person must expand the boundaries of his or her personality. The only way to do that is to break an existing coherency. If someone is shy, she can begin to change her entire personality by adopting a strong physical stance. If someone has a chip on his shoulder, he can modify his personality by tapping into his feelings of gratitude and empathy.

We tend to be creatures of language, thinking primarily in words, and we can use our verbal facility to defend our inner selves. The concepts of "lip service" and "talking the talk" point up the fact that it's easy for us to change our words without changing our behavior. However, if we modify our body language or our emotional state, true growth is more likely to happen.

I believe that the same three-domain model holds true for creativity: Creative thinking can be stimulated through techniques that are language-based, emotion-based, or movement-based.

EXPERIENCING THE RUSH

In many of my creativity training sessions, I invite my sensei (karate teacher) in to meet the class. He is able to teach everyone how to break a board with a well-placed karate chop and a very loud, from-the-gut yell. I have the members of the group write on their boards—they write down obstacles in their path, anything that is obstructing their progress or blocking their way. Then—CRACK—each of them breaks the board in two.

Reading about this, it might seem obvious ("Oh, yes, I get it; we're breaking through the barriers"), but the physical rush that each participant feels is undeniable. Again, this is why reading the exercises in this book is not a substitute for actually doing them; one provides an intellectual understanding, while the other provides a visceral understanding. Board breakers say that it requires belief, energy, and focus to break the board with their bare hands after only two or three minutes of training. It is *not* physical force. It is, in truth, the combination of faith, energy, and focus. That's it. Imagine what would happen if you applied that same intensity to the opportunities that are at hand for you.

After we've had our karate session, I ask everyone to go through the three-panel cartoon exercise, describing her thoughts before, during, and after the moment when she broke the board. It's interesting to see how the experience changes each person, even when that person thought she knew what to expect.

I recommend that, when you try some of the exercises in this chapter, you evaluate them by doing that same three-panel cartoon exercise: What did you think before, during, and after?

Now you are ready to move on to specific exercises, to indulge in a "wild and crazy time." These exercises can open the floodgates and stimulate the flow of new ideas and concepts.

BUT—

You have to do the exercises. You can't just read them and nod your head knowingly. You have to jump in with both feet and really give each exercise your best shot. Ideas will come, but only if you direct all your energy toward creating the right conditions.

You can't build muscle by just reading about exercising. You have to get your butt into the gym and really sweat. Think of these exercises as weight lifting for your creative muscles. We all have these muscles—but a lot of us have allowed them to get slack and loose.

Each of these exercises assumes that you have a problem, project, or assignment for which you need to generate new ideas. These exercises are goal-oriented in the sense that they can help you free your mind and gain a new perspective, even though, at first glance, the exercise may not deal directly with the issue at hand. With each of these exercises, think about the process, not the result.

Remember: Go through each of the steps. Don't leap ahead. Don't push to find "the right answer."

These exercises ask you to change your patterns of behavior—to allow yourself to relax, to play, to loosen up, to be silly. Changing your established way of thinking is the only way to allow those flashes of inspiration to come—we're flying kites in a storm and hoping to attract lightning.

As you're working with markers, scissors, glue, and crayons, you may wonder, "Why am I doing this?" I'll explain as we go along, but trust me, there's a method to this madness. If you commit fully, you will get results.

Pay attention to where the energy lies in the work you create. That is where the nugget of the idea that will solve your problem lies. Look for the energy, and even if the full idea isn't obvious to you, keep wondering about it, dreaming about it, writing about it, working it. An idea with energy can be fully developed . . . it's the programs without that spark of energy that are DOA.

Above all, I demand your passion.

FIRST... BREAK THE BOARD !!!

On the following page, create a list of everything that you feel is holding you back from your creative self. This can include the enemies of innovation from the second chapter, something about the way your brain works, and any physical, environmental, or preferential constraints. Take all the time you need, and don't continue on to the rest of the chapter until you've finished this exercise.

Once you have written down everything that you feel is holding you back, study the list carefully. How many of these items are manufactured excuses? How many can you eliminate by thinking in a different way?

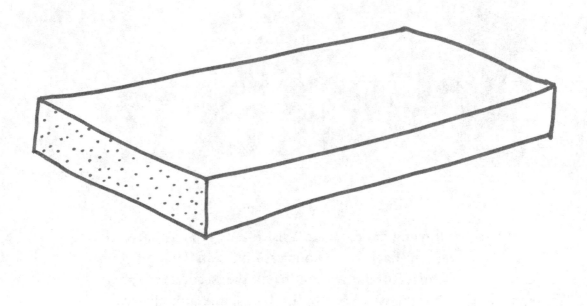

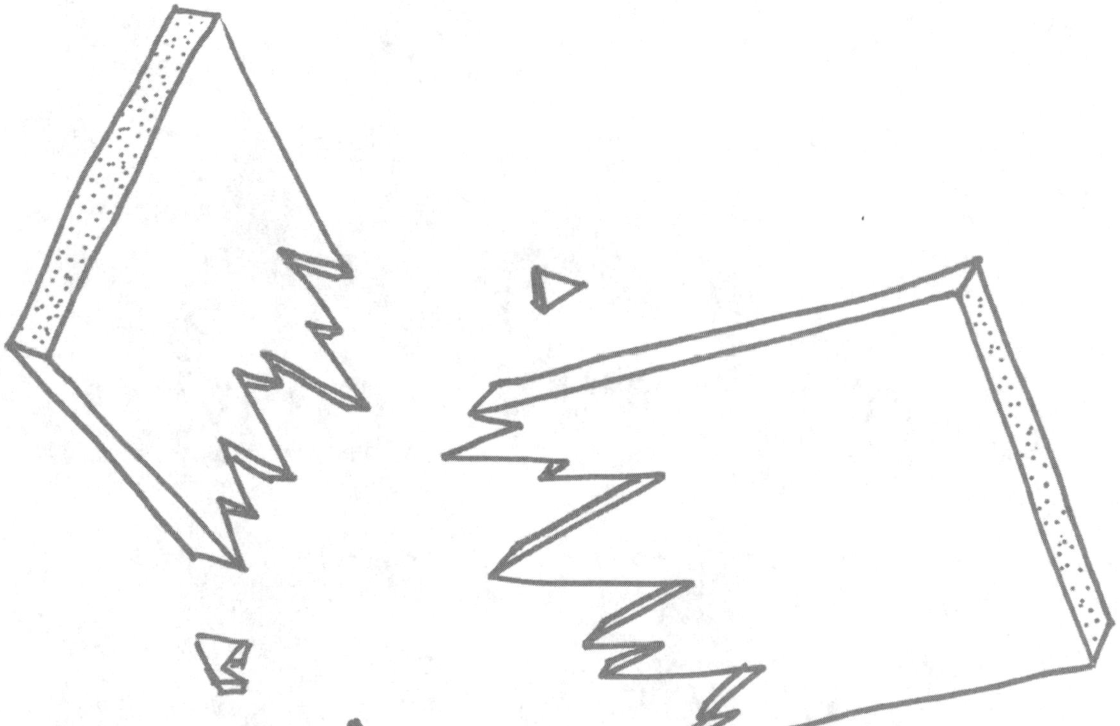

ALL RIGHT — YOU KNOW WHAT TO DO BY NOW...

RIP YOUR "BOARD" OUT OF THE BOOK!!!

RIGHT THIS MINUTE! NOW, DESTROY IT!!!

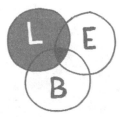 Language-Based Tools

EXERCISE

TEN RANDOM THINGS

On the next page, make a list of 10 random items—
it could be 10 things that you see while you're sitting at
your desk.

Now write as many associations as you can think of
between those things and the issue at hand.

"What does a stapler have to do with my problem?"

What are the qualities of a stapler? It binds things together, it opens up, it's something that you can use gently
or you can bang your fist on, it's something that can hide
in your drawer, it's an object of envy (how often do sta-
plers get "borrowed" permanently?), it's something that
hasn't changed much over the last 50 years . . . and so on
and so on.

As you go through this exercise with each of the 10
objects, you may stumble upon the "aha!" moment: You
see your problem in a new way.

EXERCISE

TEN RANDOM THINGS *(Continued)*

What's Going On Here ¿

Making connections between seemingly unrelated things pushes us to think about an issue in some very unexpected ways.

EXERCISE

WORD BY WORD

This is a perfect exercise for getting a small group or a team thinking together.

One person writes the beginning of a sentence and passes it to the next person. He or she adds a few words, then the next person adds a few more, and so on. (The sentence doesn't need to specifically address the problem you're working on. In fact, using a sentence that begins "Our brand personality is . . . " would defeat the spirit of the exercise.)

During the exercise, no spoken communication is allowed—let the ideas pop out in your writing. Don't restrain yourself, and don't try to push the writing in any particular direction. You'll be surprised at how quickly the group starts to think on the same wavelength.

Depending on the size of your group, you might let the page go around the circle three or four times; surprisingly enough, the writing will often come to its own natural conclusion.

EXERCISE

WORD BY WORD (Continued)

"The QUICK red elephant ran AROUND the block to FETCH a pickle."

What's Going On Here?

Discontinuous problem solving, in which each team member contributes to the outcome, establishes a group dynamic that is conducive to effective brainstorming and idea generation.

EXERCISE

NOW IT'S PERSONAL

See if you can "humanize" the situation you face in an interesting way. Give the creative problem at hand a personality and see what happens.

Is a competitor's brand like an unnoticed kid who wants tons of attention? How would you deal with that behavior in real life? What works when you're dealing with your two-year-old niece? How could you apply that knowledge to your business situation?

What's Going On Here ¿

Many business issues become so abstract that they are difficult to connect with on a visceral level. You can get a stronger grasp on a problem if you can redefine it in human terms.

Emotion-Based Tools

If you want your product or concept to really strike a chord or make a connection with someone, then it has to have an emotional, visceral quality to it. Our left brains aren't going to help us here.

We want to find a way to get around the filters that our logical left brains have put in place and tap into the creative energy of the right side of the brain. We can do this by using visual images rather than words to process information—both information coming in and information going out.

Information in: Pictures evoke emotional responses in us in a way that words can't. We respond to images viscerally, not logically. Think of photojournalism: All the words in the world can't capture the joy of a soldier kissing a girl in Times Square or the terror of a naked girl running from a napalm attack.

Information out: We're used to communicating with words, but when we speak or write, our logical left brains are in charge. We fall into established patterns. When we have to draw, most of us aren't as skilled—we don't have as many barriers getting in the way.

An important element in stimulating creativity through emotional, visual means is preparing the right environment. In other words, you need a place to play.

Get out some colored paper, markers, crayons, toys—anything that's silly, crazy, fun, and anti-"business as usual." Put on some Mozart or Bach. Change the lighting. Sit on the floor.

If you change what you're doing and how you're doing it, your thinking will change as well.

EXERCISE
MIND MAP

Begin with a circle. Write your idea (problem, issue, goal) in the circle.

Now write every related thought or idea around the circle, like moons orbiting a planet.

Don't edit yourself. Jot down your ideas as fast as they come, in any order.

EXERCISE

MIND MAP (Continued)

By laying out your ideas like this, you can often see common elements or links between concepts that you wouldn't see if you had written down your ideas in a linear, list-like way.

The mind map is a good place to begin. Your ideas are all in front of you. As with any map, you first need to know where you are.

What's Going On Here ¿

This is a way to get all your thoughts about a subject down on paper and to perceive new patterns or connections between disparate ideas.

EXERCISE
COLLAGE

Get a stack of magazines, scissors, glue, and paper.

Make a collage that evokes the essence of what you're working on.

When you've cut out the pictures, spend some time playing with them—moving them around and putting them together in different ways.

After you make the collage, put it away for a day or two, then look at it again. Sometimes you'll be surprised at what you see—something that you didn't notice when you were making it.

Show the collage to other people who don't know what inspired it. Ask them to describe their first impression—what's the first thing they think of when they see it?

What's Going On Here?

Defining a problem in purely visual terms can help to clarify the issues, revealing possible solutions or new ways to approach the problem.

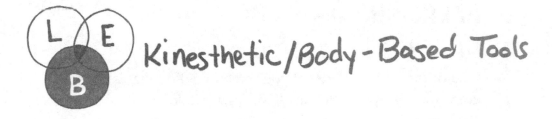

Kinesthetic/Body-Based Tools

You're facing a deadline; you've been working all day and all night. You've thought and thought and thought. Your brain is on overload; your mind is swimming with details and possibilities; and you swear you can actually feel your circuits melting down.

When your brain is frying and you've hit the wall, you need to take the pressure off your mind and let your body take over.

Rhythmic, repetitive motion of your body distracts your left brain and frees your right brain to percolate and generate new ideas. Beethoven used to do his best composing while he was walking. It's thinking while not thinking.

If you've ever had a massage, you have experienced how your mind seems to empty out; you aren't controlling it, but instead you are letting the thoughts flow by uninterrupted. It's a step toward uncorking the blockage and getting back to a freer creative flow.

EXERCISE

GET OUT

One of the best ways to get your creativity flowing is to get your endorphins flowing. Run, swim, bike, walk—in short, get outside and sweat.

EXERCISE

CONVEYOR BELT

Another method of idea generation is to produce a lot of ideas. Think of a conveyor belt or a luggage carousel, endlessly moving and bringing forth one object after another. The idea that's coming down the conveyor belt right now may not be the one you need, but the next one might be.

Pushing yourself to keep the ideas coming is a way to keep the creativity channel moving and to reduce the pressure of thinking that every idea has to be "the one."

Writing teacher Natalie Goldberg tells her students to keep the hand moving across the page, even if you're just writing "I can't think of anything new to say." Ideas lead to more ideas, which lead to even more ideas. You have to get the "bad" ideas out of the way, so that the "good" ones can emerge.

Thomas Edison, when he wasn't pondering how pinecones grow upside down, produced one minor invention every ten days and a major invention every six months. He still holds the record for number of patents: 1,093.

What's Going On Here ¿

Generating a large volume of raw content helps to eliminate the instinct to self-edit, enabling you to approach idea generation more freely.

EXERCISE

YES, BREAK THE BOARD—A REAL ONE!

Breaking boards with the guidance of a sensei, as I described at the beginning of the chapter, is a way to free your creativity through physical action. (Let me add a disclaimer here: I'm not suggesting that you go whacking away at wooden planks with your bare hands without qualified instruction. Use your common sense, folks.)

Other activities that I've had groups engage in include building fanciful prototypes of a magical music machine out of Styrofoam and Play-Doh, assembling a complete Mr. Potato Head when each participant was handed a random box of parts, and constructing towers out of Tinker Toys.

In each case, all the participants knew what they were supposed to "learn" ("Ahh, we're cooperating and working as a team!"), yet the act of physically building something by hand affected the group in a much deeper way than simply talking about the issue.

Use your hands. Build something. Make something. Break something.

Spirit-Based Tools

The last domain, where body, emotion, and language intersect, is the spiritual.

Gut feelings, instinct, a natural radar—we have all had times when we paid attention to the part of ourselves that wasn't operating on a conscious, intellectual level. It was deeper, more grounded, more certain. It's difficult to always be plugged in to this part of ourselves—our essential selves—but when the connection is there, it's strong and sure.

I believe that meditation and dreaming are the keys to unlocking what our essential self knows in a way that we cannot do through our normal, waking intellect.

If you think back to the enemies of innovation, the common element of all of them was some form of fear. When we strengthen ourselves, becoming more connected and in tune with who we really are and what our goals are, we are less likely to fall prey to paralyzing fear. We think more clearly; we are more open and perceptive. We can really see.

EXERCISE

KEEP BREATHING

Meditation is a fantastic way of suppressing the left brain and focusing our creativity.

I'd like you to experiment with sitting and paying attention to your breath for two minutes upon waking and before sleeping every day for a week.

Sit with your feet flat on the floor, either cross-legged on the floor or on an armless chair. Sit straight, with your ears over your shoulders over your hips. Feel the area about two inches below your navel. Inhale into this place. When you inhale, your belly should expand. When you exhale, your belly should contract.

(Keep your belly soft and pliable. This is not the time to "hold it in." No one's looking.)

Count "one" as you breathe in; count "two" as you breathe out. Then count "three" as you breathe in and "four" as you breathe out. Keep going up to ten, then start over at one. If your mind wanders and you find yourself thinking about something else, gently start over at one. If you realize suddenly that you're on thirty-six, gently start over at one.

When a thought comes, thank it for showing up, then let it go. Thoughts should appear and disappear like clouds on a blue sky. Always bring your attention back to rest lightly on your breath.

EXERCISE

KEEP BREATHING (Continued)

Record in your journal what you experience. It may be nothing at first. You may be resistant in the beginning. Just keep at it, learn heuristically, and see what unfolds in front of you.

EXERCISE

BEYOND MEDITATION

There are many ways to engage your spiritual self beyond simple meditation and dreams. You have to follow your instinct in choosing a path that is right for you.

You might try a guided meditation: Meet your older, wiser self on a trail, and ask for guidance in your current situation.

Or ask your Higher Power for help. Prayer is another form of meditation.

Or go to a spiritual service of some kind.

Or help someone else for an hour or two. Tutor a kid. Feed the homeless. Get outside of yourself and your concerns. Making a Copernican Shift in your own life can be a step toward releasing the flow of creative energy.

# 7 MEASURING THE VOLTAGE

You've made the leap, taken the chances, put yourself out there . . . and now you're reaching the end of the journey of getting in touch with your innate creativity. And yet, it's not so much a journey as a cycle, an experience that you'll have again and again now that you know how. As you generate high-voltage ideas during these cycles of creativity, you need some way to gauge those ideas, to choose among them, to measure their effectiveness before you send them out into the world. That's what this chapter is about.

So, you've been through the journey toward creating a high-voltage idea. You've avoided the enemies of ideas; you've asked questions, identified areas of potential energy, shifted your viewpoint, and generated possible solutions.

Now what?

Now it's time to assess the power of the ideas you've come up with—which of them are high-voltage ideas, and which barely have enough juice to fire up a 40-watt bulb?

In the first chapter, we talked about the zing, the electric charge that a good idea has that springs from a combination of relevance and difference. How do you measure the zing?

OPTIMAL EXPERIENCE

In my exploration of creativity and the creative process, I've studied the work of Mihaly Csikszentmihaly (pronounced "chik-SENT-me-high"), especially his theories of optimal experience.

He describes the state of "flow": the state we are in when we are completely absorbed in what we're doing, when we are unaware of the passage of time, when our abilities are perfectly matched to the task at hand. He created a graph that measures the difficulty of the activity along the x axis and personal skill along the y axis. When difficulty is high and skills are low, frustration results; when skills are high and difficulty is low, you see boredom. But when both skills and ability are high, the subject experiences flow.

I discussed this method of quantifying experience with Professor Csikszentmihaly. I was curious to see if a similar approach could be used to measure the "voltage" of an idea or a concept.

Instead of skill level and difficulty, I created a graph in which the axes measure the uniqueness of an idea and its relevance. If an idea is very relevant, but doesn't rate very high in uniqueness or difference, then you have consumer boredom: "I can use it, but so what; it's the same old thing." If the opposite is true—an idea is distinctive, but it doesn't have a clear application to real life—then we're in "too crazy for me" territory.

But when an idea is highly relevant *and* fresh, then the consumer response reaches the high-voltage zone.

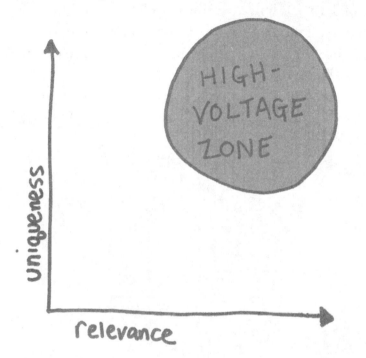

MAPPING THE RESPONSE

So, there you are, surrounded by all the ideas that you and your team have generated. The usual post-brainstorming process of going around the room and voting thumbs-up or thumbs-down on each new idea (or dissecting and discussing the life out of each one) puts you in danger of falling back into the logic-versus-energy trap: "That seems like a good idea, but

I know the VP won't see it that way. You had to have been here . . . "

Instead, pinpoint where each idea falls on the voltage graph. On a scale of 1 to 10, how unique or new is the idea? On a scale of 1 to 10, how relevant is it? Does it address the consumer conflict? Is it bringing resolution to a paradox? Then graph your results. Those in the upper left area of the grid will typically be the ideas with the most zing!

When you see the ideas arranged on the graph, it will be clear which ones fall into the zone and which fall by the wayside.

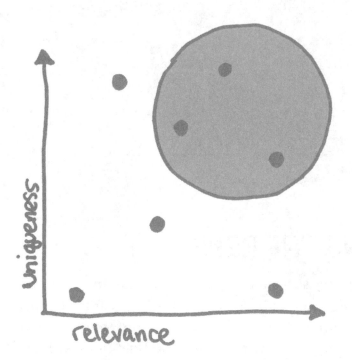

ASK THE EXPERTS

When I'm going through this process, I then take the new concepts back to the experts: consumers like the ones I interviewed at the beginning. I give them questionnaires that basically ask, "Is this idea new, or is it the same old thing?" "Would you use this every day, or is it 'just good for camping'?"

This works with moms, with kids, with teens, with 'tweens—anyone you could possibly want to ask. They can tell you, "Well, my mom would use it, but it's not cool enough for me and my friends," or, "My kids would go crazy for it, but it's kind of far out for me." "That's interesting." "That's wild." "That's cool." "I've seen that before." "BORING!" "Lame!"

When you've hit the zone, you'll know it. With a high-voltage idea, there's no indifference. "Oh, well" is banished. There's real excitement as potential energy is released.

With this kind of evaluation, remember that you're dealing with human beings, not with a Geiger counter. It's best not to overload your experts with too many variations on an idea. You want to see how one idea stands or falls on its own merits. Don't fall into the trap of conducting a popularity poll: "Which of these five ideas is the best?" Comparing ideas is not the same as learning about each one in depth.

Also, don't be too quick to discard ideas that get initial bad responses. Remember the concept of "never say no." Your respondent might just be in his or her own analytical mode, telling you that "that could never work" rather than actually having a personal response ("I hate everything that's lemon-scented, because I'm allergic.") You always want to ask the question, *why*? A forcefully negative response at least has energy, in contrast to a tepid "Yeah, it's okay, I guess" response.

SAMPLE QUESTIONNAIRE FOR KIDS

Idea Name: _____ Group #: _____

I'd say this idea is exciting for:
( ) little kids
( ) me
( ) older kids

This idea is:
( ) boring
( ) cool
( ) wacko

The kind of store that would have a program like this is:
( ) nowhere I want to go
( ) where I gotta go
( ) where I'd go if I had to

If I saw this idea on TV, I'd:
( ) pay attention
( ) mute it
( ) change the channel

I could understand this idea:
( ) right away
( ) after I saw the drawings
( ) I still don't get it

SAMPLE QUESTIONNAIRE FOR MOMS

Idea Name: _____   Group #: _____

I'd say this idea is right for:
- ( ) when I was growing up
- ( ) my family and my kids
- ( ) when my kids have kids

My kid would say this idea is:
- ( ) lame
- ( ) cool
- ( ) crazy

This idea is:
- ( ) creative for creativity's sake
- ( ) same old, same old
- ( ) fresh and interesting

This idea seems:
- ( ) like it would add variety to my routine
- ( ) boring and mainstream
- ( ) too far out

Compared to other products I see, this idea is:
- ( ) way too wacky
- ( ) same stuff, new name
- ( ) something different that I actually think I'd like

This makes me think of the manufacturer:
- ( ) in the same way I always have
- ( ) as out of its mind
- ( ) in a fresh, interesting way

THE ANSWERS AT THE BACK OF THE BOOK

Return with me to where this story began: with me, the "not creative" one, painting a mural on the basement wall, trying to keep up with my sister.

There are always going to be times when each of us is put into a similar situation, whether we believe ourselves to be creative or not. You're handed a brush, put in front of a cement wall, and told to "do something new," when all around you it seems as if everyone else has better ideas than you do. Substitute a PowerPoint presentation and a client's conference room for the brush and the basement wall, and I'm sure the setup sounds all too familiar.

I wrote this book to give you a process that you can rely on in those situations. The thing to remember is that this is a process, a series of actions that can lead you to a solution. Every time I work with a new client, I get nervous, because I have no idea what the winning idea is. But the answer always comes, in one way or another, when my clients and I go through the process together.

When we go through the process, we have to momentarily set aside logic, face our fears, and try to think in a new way, to connect with a different part of ourselves. The concepts that the exercises are based on can be very disconcerting when you're used to thinking in an orderly, sequential way; the way you feel is unfamiliar, different, unquantifiable. You may think, how can I get anything out of this if the end result isn't predetermined? Where are the answers at the back of the book?

Remember that you're not abandoning your left brain; you're just putting it on hold for a moment. The feeling is a bit like swinging out into the void on a trapeze or stepping off the high dive. There are no guardrails. It's a rush of adrenaline—an invigorating or terrifying feeling, depending on your point of view.

But if you go through the process often enough, the feeling will become familiar. You can develop your intuitive side along with your analytical side. You can become used to the idea that although there is a reliable method that you can use, the outcome is different every time. What I hope happens is that you surprise yourself.

The last thing I'll leave you with is to remember the Copernican Shift. Too often, I get the feeling that books on topics like this by "experts" and "authorities" are at the center of their own little universes, flinging out their pronouncements and rules to all the readers who are orbiting them like an asteroid belt.

I'd like you to think of it in the opposite way: You, of course, are at the center. This book is one of the many things orbiting you, to be useful at the right time and place: when you are blocked by the enemies of ideas; when you need to ask new questions; when you need the jolt of a high-voltage idea.

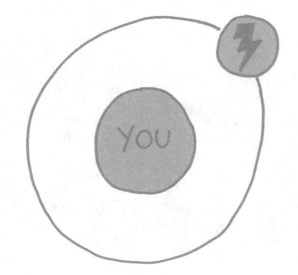

EXERCISE

THREE-PANEL CARTOON

You didn't think you were going to get away so easily, did you? There's one more exercise, and it's my favorite.

Draw a three-panel (before-during-after) cartoon of your experience with this book as a whole, especially considering the shift in your feelings about your creativity. Include your thought bubbles and a title for each panel.

What's Going On Here ¿

You've made it through this journey, and now you're free! Creatively free, that is. I hope your experience was a great one, and that the "after" panel depicts a new confidence in your innate creative skills. Add a "future" panel, if you like, showing the way your career success (and personal success) can only increase when you apply these new ways of thinking.

INDEX

ABOUT THE AUTHOR

Kay Allison is founder of The Energy Annex, a marketing innovation and consulting firm that shows clients including Avon, Kraft Foods, Nestlé, and others how to create new, revenue-generating ideas. Allison is the executive in residence for Northwestern University's graduate Integrated Marketing Communications program and has been quoted in leading publications including the *Los Angeles Times*, *Investor's Business Daily*, the *Chicago Sun-Times*, and the *Economist*.